The Best I Remember

A Cruel British Tragedy

The author wishes to thank *Angela Bailey* for her editing, proofreading, and book designing. Thank you for believing in my story *Angela*, may you rest in peace.

Cover Design: Angela Bailey
Front Cover Photos: HMS Aquitania, public domain, State Library of South Australia Passenger list, Canadian Museum of Immigration at Pier 21, Halifax, Nova Scotia, Fairbridge Farm School, Duncan, BC, photographer unknown

The Best I Remember – A Cruel British Tragedy - Copyright 2021 by Tom Isherwood

Copyright © 2021 Tom Isherwood
All rights reserved.
ISBN: 9781777695903

The Best I Remember

A Cruel British Tragedy

Tom Isherwood

ACKNOWLEDGMENTS

The memory of my lost childhood is always there to remind me that I was robbed of my God-given childhood. At age eighty, I am so tired when thinking of the neglect of many Child Migrants who were alone and exiled from their homeland and all family. I have to thank some unknown power for giving me the will to survive despite the unknown fear that stained my young heart.

I am thankful for the love of my wife and children, and all those that genuinely care about me today and all those years gone by. I would also like to thank Rita Lemmi and Cindy Gendron for their assistance and encouragement in helping me put my story in writing.

To Kathy Tomlinson from CBC for investigating the truth and her efforts in arranging funding through International Social Services for our trip to the UK.

I say to the governments of the United Kingdom and Canada, thank you for nothing. Canada has tried everything possible to hide or distort Child Migrant history after giving the 'thumbs up' to receive 28 forgotten children, plus another 6 children who were shipped the following year.

ABOUT THE AUTHOR

Thomas Isherwood is a Child Migrant who was born on December 23, 1938, in Birmingham, England.

With the start of the Second World War in 1939, a consequential chain of events placed Tom as an 8-year-old boy on a rugged journey throughout life. No human should ever have to endure the cruelty, punishment, and loneliness that Tom's birth country placed on him, as well as many other children. For Tom, the majority of his baby years were spent in orphanages or emigration homes in England that dealt with the trafficking of children. Tom does not remember his mother or father, and one document even suggested, *"The boy forget about his entire past in England."*[1] Everything appeared fine until his mind began to wonder, leaving an unsteady feeling within, telling him that something was not quite right.

"The Best I Remember" tells of Tom's struggle as a young boy to survive all alone in a foreign land, even after, surviving the war and all that came with it. For the most part, the sadness Tom grew up with was blocked and locked out of his heart and mind, too painful to recall. Through all of Tom's young years not a soul knew how he truly felt, as children were seen, not heard. Tom, along with the other 27 children and two adults were shipped here and there like animals, with no comfort or concerns for their overall wellbeing.

Over fifty years had gone by until the British barrel of lies sprang a leak. Through a maze of disbelief and lost confusion, a large family that Tom never knew existed began to surface, leading to a reunion in England, Wales, and Australia with siblings and family that shared the same blood that ran through his very veins. They entered his life for such a short time with so much love, sadness, and emotion, it was difficult on the human framework. Today, all he now has are those few memories of that short time together, and they will forever be cherished. This happy reunion however, left Tom feeling bittersweet for it led another part of his heart to ache as he wondered how England could do such harm to their own children, at the very least they could have kept brothers and sisters together; instead, they shipped them off to separate continents. Eventually, England was caught in their lies and questions were raised; sadly, they lied to the world and refused to correspond with Tom, leaving him to this day, still trying to untie the knots from their ugly past. The flames of his horrible story have died; however, the embers will forever, continue to smolder.

---

1. Original document scanned and provided on page 147

CONTENTS

Author's Note	1
Preface	2
Chapter One: Reporters 1999	5
Chapter Two: Telling the Truth	7
Chapter Three: Memories of Fairbridge Farm School	14
Chapter Four: Tommy Lovick	23
Chapter Five: Newton	30
Chapter Six: Boys' Home	34
Chapter Seven: Tap Dancing	37
Chapter Eight: The Skelton's	39
Chapter Nine: The Marshall's	43
Chapter Ten: Bob	49
Chapter Eleven: Royal Canadian Air Force	52
Chapter Twelve: Mr. Berkefield	57
Chapter Thirteen: The Yukon	59
Chapter Fourteen: Sheryl	65
Chapter Fifteen: Shocking News	68
Chapter Sixteen: Canadian Citizen	70
Chapter Seventeen: Reconnecting	75
Chapter Eighteen: Back to London	90
Chapter Nineteen: Pat, 2001	95
Chapter Twenty: Pier 21	96
Today is March 25, 2001	99
July 20, 2001	102
Chapter Twenty-One: CBC	105
Family Reunion- Wales	107
Wales	109
Middlemore Homes, August 21st	112

Fairbridge-London, August 22nd	114
Health Committee Visit	115
January 25, 2002 – After Health Office Fiasco	116
Trip to Bristol Bay	118
After Bristol Bay	118
Caravan Park	119
September 20, 2002 – Brother Joe Visit to Canada	120
On the Road from the Airport	121
Sep 30, 2002 – Meeting My Perfect Canadian Family	121
Sep 30, 2002	123
October 1st, 2002 – Leaving Osoyoos	123
Harrison Hot Springs	124
Stave Lake Power Dam	125
The Train and the Harbor	127
Lions Gate Bridge	128
Bob the Bus Driver	129
Quay in North Vancouver	130
Goodbye and Farewell	130
Leaving on a Jet Plane	131
Present Time	133
Fairbridge History	134
Acquired Sixty Years Too Late	136
Poetry	163

AUTHOR'S NOTE

My name is Tom Isherwood. I grew up with many uncertainties in my life; my exact birthday, where my parents/siblings were, what happened to them, and where I belonged. Most times, I felt I did not even know who I was; after all, everything I had ever known was stripped from my fingertips and left in the burning of my past. It was not until the creation of my own family that who I am, became clear. I am a husband to a loving wife, a father to beautiful children, a grandfather and great grandfather to the adventurous little and not so little ones, and I am a friend to the lovely souls who have entered my life throughout this journey. From playing in the water, to ping pong and pool, the enjoyment I receive from laughing with my family is one that will fill my heart forever. A heart that for a long time I did not know I had. I began asking questions at a young age about my past, and how what happened to me was allowed.

I'm now 82, still left asking questions which appear to have no answers, or at least none that the government is willing to share. After England told me to "go home" and Canada claimed I did not exist on immigration records, I felt hopelessly lost. I got so tired of the rejection and locked doors that only the people responsible seemed to have the key for. There are still many days where my heart aches with pain and I'll forever long for the truth that is hidden from history; however, I feel I have some unknown power to thank for giving me the will to survive the blanket of fear that stained my young heart; but with that, it is thanks to my immediate family that I must give for providing me the will to survive the adulthood that followed. I thank my wife Sheryl, who has loved and looked after me for the past 58 years. I also thank our children and their children, our four grandsons and four great grandchildren for unlocking the word love and placing it in my heart. My past was filled with loneliness, pain, and heartbreak from the actions that were inflicted upon me ever since a young age, and although that will never change, the ones in my life today have allowed light to shine through the darkness, and I thank them for being the reason I stand here and can share this story with you today.

PREFACE

The year 2001 was my first attempt at putting my journey as a British Child Migrant down on paper. My reason for writing is that a chain of events have taken place that many may find absolutely unbelievable, and in the 90's, those events began to unravel. Controlled by the homes for so-called orphans in England starting around 1943, I was shipped to Canada in 1947 at the age of eight, and then shipped across the country to endure more orphan homes throughout my youth. At the age of sixty-two, in the year 2001, I experienced the worst nightmare of all. I did not exist. There were no government records from my birth in 1938 to 1947 in England, and none in Canada from 1947 to 1955. Specifically, Canada denied my existence here on August 12, 1992, as immigration staff concluded I was not a Canadian Citizen. Apparently, I had been separated from a very large family and it was suggested to me that a clerical error had taken place. Their official response to this dilemma was in other words, "too bad so sad for the little lad". I was determined to find out the truth and gain access to records that I knew must exist. Unfortunately, each time I inquired about my past it seemed that all the doors were being slammed in my face. Politicians and newspapers would run and hide at the sound of the Isherwood name and were rude beyond reproach.

As the years rolled by my search did not get any easier. I felt like the flames inside of me would die but the embers would forever continue to smolder. My hope was that – like the Olympic Torch – the cruelty of these war crimes against the children of England would one day, light up the world.

Many years have passed since the year 2001 when I was introduced at my place of work to a strange machine called a computer and began documenting my thoughts. This caused my memory to flash back to the school days of grade six or seven when I decided to master a typewriter, or so I thought. As I sat in the classroom for my very first lesson, I noticed just one other boy in the room. I faintly remember the teacher going through procedures to familiarize us young students with our individual typewriter. The time came to write, and it all began with the words, "The quick brown fox jumped over the lazy dog." The other boy was long finished typing that simple line while the clickety-clack of my machine continued. I quickly learned to despise that noise. The teacher softly, but firmly, told me typing was not for me; and with that, I never looked back.

The year 2001 would challenge my two-finger typing once again. It all started when my friend Rita, a work colleague, happened to look over my shoulder when my two-finger typing was active, creating words joined together with no punctuation. After reading the mess upon the page Rita looked at me in disbelief. Never knowing a thing about my past brought tears to her eyes. I needed help. I will never forget Rita and the friendship she showed me in getting my story onto the computer. One rainy day with down time at my workplace, I had the opportunity and freedom to practice my computer skills with the hope of defeating that shiny, but knowledgeable know-it-all tin can. I knew I had a story my two fingers needed to write; the story of an eight-year-old Tom Isherwood, the boy who survived the Second World War with perfect attendance.

When I began to ask questions in hopes of filling in the blanks of why I suffered such a lost, unloved childhood, I soon found out that all files concerning my life were sealed or erased. The blood within my body boiled, fuelled by the lies that suppressed my story of a young child of war. It was time for the truth to be told. The truth was that the Government of Canada refused to recognize or acknowledge their part in stripping myself and many others of our childhoods. Even into our adulthood as I soon came to realize, they failed to admit their part in this horrendous history. No acknowledgment and no apologies. This left it up to me and my two fingers to tell my truth – the truth of the forgotten children of war. This book is dedicated to a group of 28 kids that were shipped like sheep to slaughter, over a vast ocean, to a strange land in 1947. Most of us shared a similar fate in Canada, even after surviving the biggest war in history back in England.

My wish is that all of the kids turned out okay and had a reasonable life. I guarantee their hearts and souls felt, and may still feel, the loveless holes left by a childhood of loneliness. I am sure many of them would agree that life can feel like a relentless, losing battle for a Child Migrant. The people that could have helped were seemingly, too busy filling their own faces and wallets to bother with this embarrassing tragedy from the past. Imagine growing up without knowing your family (or forgetting that you even had one), nor receiving any emotional love, support, or stability in your life; and thus, not ever knowing the feeling of bonding. This is an experience I wish no child ever has to endure.

CHAPTER ONE: REPORTERS 1999

In 1999 a local Vancouver newspaper, *The Province*, had published an article about how the British quit shipping children to Canada after 1939. I knew this information was wrong, so I sent the reporter a message to point out this untruth. The reporter contacted me and when he arrived at my home, he was amazed at the information I had gathered and the story I would tell him. The article appeared in the *Sunday Province* on February 07, 1999, and this would start a chain reaction of events.

I soon received a phone call from a retired British newspaperman, living on Salt Spring Island with forty-seven years in the business. He proclaimed that he alone could help me reunite with my family. It turned out that he used the *Sunday Province's* story but had to black out the pictures of myself and family members to avoid being sued by the photographer. The sly old fellow then faxed his newfound prize to *The London Times* newspaper in London, England. He had conned me. On February 10th, I received a call from *The London Times* at my place of work. The woman sounded so excited – and quite frankly, so was I. Another call came the next day from *The London Times* asking for my permission to investigate the story further and to reproduce pictures or documents they might find. I sent permission by fax immediately. My heart was bursting, and I felt truly thankful for the attention these people were going to bring to this historic matter. They asked if they could send a photographer to my residence for pictures, as this whole thing was incredible and terribly exciting. Photos were taken of me here in Canada and also of my supposed siblings in Australia.

The Times said they had spoken to my siblings in Australia. Tension mounted as we wondered what might happen. On February 12th, yet another phone call from an English newspaper, *The Mail on Sunday*. They said things were progressing smoothly and not to worry. On February 17th, I talked with *The London Times,* and they again assured me that things were on track. But, on March 18th, 1999, when I phoned the newspaper in England and left a message, they did not return my call. I thought I would try to contact them one last time on April 5th, and it was this phone call that made me realize, this was going nowhere. The pressure of all that had happened was enormous and difficult to handle. Knowing the truth and having the truth told, was so important to me.

I decided to call the reporter from Salt Spring Island who forwarded the story to the *Times* to see if he knew anything. He seemed more interested in telling me they had paid him enough for possibly his last visit home to the old country. Also, knowing that I worked for Corrections Canada, he had the nerve to ask if I could feed him inside information, especially about English Inmates doing time in a Canadian Federal Institution. I told him, "Thanks for nothing! Get lost." I never heard from the old fart again. My distrust for the English was now greatly enhanced. I knew they must've realized the harm they'd done to their own children, and this news was not something they wanted to share.

CHAPTER TWO: TELLING THE TRUTH

There have been several books written about the thousands of British Child Migrants that were shipped to Australia years after the Second World War was over. *Why? Why did this happen?* A 1998 report by the British Parliament's Select Committee on Health stated that, "Child migration was often seen to be of economic benefit, both to Britain (because it relieved the burden on public finances of looking after these children) and to the receiving countries (because child migrants were seen as being potential members of a healthy and well-trained work force)." [2] A member of the British Parliament at the time said, "We must get the diseased tissue off the streets of England".[3] Another suggested reason for the Child Migrant scheme was to populate the colonies with 'good British white stock'. [4]

The committee's report quoted a former child migrant describing how "on arrival in Fremantle, Australia, he and the other children were greeted by a senior clergyman who said, "We need white stock. We need this country to be populated by white stock because we are terrified of the Asian hordes."[3] One of the frustrating untruths that the British Government have stated (and written in the *House of Commons Health Committee Third Report* as recently as July 1998) is that Child Migration from Britain to Canada was NOT resumed after the Second World War.

I am living proof that this is a bold-faced lie. According to a program I watched on television, not only did the British Home Office know about the sinister abuse and heartbreak of their own babies, so did the Royal Family.[5] The government stated in a report, "It is not desirous to separate the children". What they failed to say was that only applied for the children of rich families who moved Heaven and Earth to shield their children from the horrors of war. Nobody gave two shits about kids with names like Beryl, Margaret, Janet, Tommy, or Joseph Isherwood. Their report goes on to say, "The history of child migration in Australia is in many ways a history of lies and deceit." I would like the world to know that Canada also played a part in this massive cover up of violated human rights.

---

2.   Apology Opens Wounds of British Migrant Program, By John F. Burns Nov. 22, 2009, *New York Times*
3.   British House of Commons Hansard, May 1999
4.   Liverpool University Archives, 0.296: Archives of the Fairbridge Society [hereinafter cited as Liverpool-Fairl]ridge Archives], 17/1, ''Canadian Government Departments-summaries and reports on relations between the government and Fairbridge"; Lumley, typescript notes of interviews [1934], p. 1.
5.   *The Queen's First Ever Speech 1940 Was About Child Migrants*, Louise Ridley *The Huffington Post* UK 20150908

I am a British Child Migrant that was shipped to Canada on the troop ship *HMS Aquitania* with twenty-seven other migrant kids in May of 1947. Many years would go by before the pieces of this broken puzzle would surface. Indeed, some of those kids whom I shared the bomb shelter with in England were my real sisters and brother. I had no knowledge of this for many years. All four of my siblings were sent to Australia several years after I was sent to Canada. Coldly and heartlessly, I was separated from all of my family with no explanation. Some documents indicate that perhaps, the terrible mistake was recognized but it was too late by then and the damage to my young life was done. I was born on December 23rd (or 25th) in 1938 on British soil in the district of Yardley, a suburb of the City of Birmingham. No one seemed sure of the date so the 23rd was chosen. Apparently, I was baptized a Catholic but Canada accepted only Protestants where I was going, so that is what they said I was. At that time and age, what did I know? Kids did what they were told and were to be seen and not heard. Besides, as a young boy, I would have just viewed the whole thing as a big adventure.

In the year 2000 I found out that I had a sister that was shipped to Australia that was born in September of 1938. *Could that have been possible?* Over fifty-five years had gone by since my journey on the *Aquitania*. I will now attempt to tell my story of a Canadian Child Migrant, abused and exiled illegally from his country of birth – to tell the truth, as best I can remember.

* * *

Nine months after I entered the world, Britain declared war on Germany. I have no memory of living with my parents except for faint and distant pictures of big people making a lot of noise and a dim picture in my clouded memory of a dreary building that could have been my home. I really did not know what a war was, so I can only write from documents, my memory, and my heart about when I was a child of war. I have been asked many times over the years if I was scared. The answer is always, "No". War should be scary, and it is. But if that is all you have known; it becomes part of your life. Like a little fawn born in the forest, one of the first lessons is that of survival – listen and identify all the different sounds and smells that fill the air. That is what we instinctively did as children too. Most of all, just as a fawn knows, pay attention to your teacher, the mother who loves you and would sacrifice her life for you. God's creatures that hesitate are lost, so instincts become sharp in order to survive.

The will to survive was built in and would keep me safe. As safe as could be from predators along my journey on the path of life. The war raged on, days turned into weeks, and then months and years went by. The sounds of war were constant, and the devastation and rubble from the bombing were a reminder of what hell might look like. I would play in the rubble and debris of a particular bombed out building. I recall looking out a massive hole in a wall while other kids would be yelling, "Come out! The devil lives in there". I do not remember where I was, but that picture has been in my mind forever. Sometimes, as a child, I would wake up in a cold sweat; pictures of a Fagin-like man chasing me with false teeth in his outstretched hands. He would just about catch me, and then the dream that was larger than life, would end. In 1943 I was placed in a home for the 'under privileged' with many other children, or so old documents claim. Middlemore Homes was an Emigration Home that was in the baby business. At five years of age, I was a veteran of this battle-scarred country.

Middlemore was a huge brick building. There was another building, the Crowley House, directly behind where the babies lived until they were mobile enough to exist in the main building. The basement of Middlemore served as the bomb shelter, where we spent many hours singing and praying at the direction of the adults. One day, a bomb hit Middlemore and one wing of the building was destroyed. Being so young, I knew nothing of the casualties. To me, it seemed like a normal day. When the 'all-clear' was given, we went out to the pasture where Babs the dapple horse and Billy the goat lived. They did not seem agitated by the day's events or by their surroundings, We picked dandelion leaves from the field and returned them to a big grey tub filled with water, the same tub that now and then we kids would bob for apples in. The apples would float in the tub full of water and we would try to pull one out using only our teeth. I recall fun and laughter, as I remember bobbing for apples. After the dandelion leaves were washed, they were placed between dry bread with hard cheese and we would eat vigorously, as if it were a royal feast.

There was an old bike called a Penny Farthing that had a really high wheel on the front and two little ones on the back, sort of like an oversized tricycle. The bigger kids made us push them because they could not reach the pedals. I don't remember any fighting between the children, probably because any form of disobedience was not accepted. I cannot remember my brother or sisters being in the home, as the old documents suggest. I was just another kid in a home with a lot of other kids. We lived by a routine of strict discipline and were taught many things to do with survival while the war raged on. Even going to the bomb shelter was practiced with precision many, many times. We were all like brothers and sisters and would not realize the extent of our plight till many years later.

I attended school, as children started at the age of five years old. We walked to school and a deep part of my memory tells me we passed a huge spooky-looking cemetery. I remember huge iron gates at the entrance and a matching fence with pointed tips that reached towards the sky. Every day there were things going on there, and we were frightened of the men dressed in black who were the gravediggers. Many processions entered the mighty gates and were swallowed up by the feelings of sadness and death in the air, and the heavy swirls of mist and fog. We would run faster than the wind to get by that dreadful place.

The hair on my head bristled and my young body would turn cold and clammy with fear. There was no alternate way to pass this drab, scary place and we believed the gravediggers wanted to bury us alive. This memory lives on in me many, many years later. I do not have any photos of me at Middlemore Homes, school or anywhere else that I may have lived during that time. I only have the collection of images saved by my own memory. I faintly remember swinging between two classroom desks, slipping and cutting my ear. The cut required attention and several stitches at a hospital. There were big white globe lights hanging down from the ceiling and someone was fussing over me. I carry the small scar behind my left ear as a reminder of so long ago.

Sometimes we would 'scrum' apples from an orchard we passed. Green as the apples were, we ate even the core and I don't recall ever getting a bellyache. I liked school and did well, according to my first report card which I viewed for the first time in 2001 (over fifty years later). Someone took some of us children to a movie once, which I never forgot the title of – *George Formby and his Motor Bike*. These younger years were okay. After all, what did I know about life? Years later, rumors claimed that we children were drugged at Middlemore

Homes to quell our memories of the horrid time we went through. It is said that at a young age, children were sent to work in factories and businesses owned by the Cadbury Family. John Cadbury was Chairman of the Board at Middlemore Homes for 25 years and definitely would have had his finger on the pulse and corruption that went on.

How could I have known that the institution was preparing me for the horror that awaited me down my path of life? The War was easy. We children never started it, but we paid extreme penalties. As adults, we continue to endure the shockwaves created by the monsters that orchestrated our exile so long ago. To this very day, records and pictures of my young life, from birth in 1938 to 1955 are virtually non-existent. England and Canada have kept the postwar Canadian Child Migrants a secret for too long. If the truth could be told, England would have to face its own war crimes against their own babies.

* * *

As I write, my mind strains to bring back some semblance of reality from my young life. I struggle for words to describe the fragmented pictures that surface now and then in the dusty library of my mind. I try to make sense of the scraps of the limited information that squeeze out of my overloaded mind about a terrible past. I have struggled for over fifty years with no help or understanding from the people that did this to me. To rob me of my childhood and family forever is a crime, and the world should know about this sick British and Canadian tragedy that has been hidden for so many years.

* * *

In May of 1947, I was placed on a train going somewhere. My memory of this train ride is fuzzy but becomes clearer when I boarded the troop ship *Aquitania* in the British port of Southampton. I have since heard that the *Aquitania* was the third largest and most rat-infested ship in the fleet. Once aboard the ship with twenty-seven other kids we learned that we were heading to a place called Canada.

I remember the soldiers on board would give us chocolate bars and treated us kindly. I was sailing across the North Atlantic Ocean without a care in the world. My memory of the long crossing is dim. I did not consider my destiny at the time, as this was beyond the scope of my young mind. Besides, children were not in a position to ask questions.

I remember running on the huge decks of the *Aquitania* and looking at the huge mountains of waves the ship had to slice through. There was no land in sight and the only sound was of the powerful sea. Crossing the Atlantic was rough, but it was quite an adventure for a young boy. Some British children were shipped to Canada before the War got into full swing. This was to save them from the horrors that kids like me were subjected to. After the war, they got to go home to their Mummies and Daddies. Little buggers like me who were still living in the homeland, were experimenting with the machines of war and the devastation and unknown sadness that war had handed us. We were then kicked out of our country of birth after the war, while the country shipped the privileged children back to England.

Little did I know then, but my very own family protested violently to my disappearance. They inquired as to my whereabouts but were denied the truth. On May 25, 1947, the *Aquitania* docked without mishap in Halifax, Nova Scotia in Canada with twenty-eight British migrant children on its manifest. Many years later this would be denied, as would our existence. We eventually boarded a Canadian Pacific Railway train pulled by powerful steam locomotives. They were a beautiful sight to behold. The 'all aboard' was given and the tons of iron flexed their muscles and started us on another journey. Smoke billowed overhead and I remember the shrill whistle of the train. The train ride seemed to go on forever and I had never seen sights as I did out of that coach window.

The train rolled by a forever-changing countryside filled with mountains, lakes, rivers, streams, and animals that I could not identify or imagine. There were waterfalls, canyons, and tunnels through solid rock. I had a million questions to ask, but nobody to answer them. Life seemed exciting and I did not have a care in the world. From the Atlantic Ocean in the East to the Pacific Ocean in the West, the powerful engines roared through the day and night. Somehow, I had been chosen to leave Hell for Heaven – at least it appeared that way.

* * *

As I grew older more cracks would appear and I would ask God to help me understand these adult people that had deceived me and set the stage for many years of sexual and mental cruelty. They robbed me of my family, my childhood, and of love and belonging.

* * *

Five days later we arrived on the West Coast of Canada in the city of Vancouver, Province of British Columbia. From there it was on to a ferryboat that took us across the Pacific Ocean waters to a place called Vancouver Island. We got off the ferryboat when it docked in Victoria, the Capital City of British Columbia. We had crossed about 38 miles of water that separated us from the mainland. Next, we were on a bus to our new home at Prince of Wales Fairbridge Farm School near the town of Duncan.

I cannot remember everything perfectly, but I do remember getting off the bus and seeing some awfully big boys. It turned out that most of them had come to Fairbridge before the war and were much older and bigger than our group, they appeared to be giving us the once over. They were not the lucky ones who were sent back after the war. After all I had been through at already such a young age, not much could phase me, including the bigger boys. I was probably the youngest and the smallest at Fairbridge at that time. It turned out that the older boys did not associate with us 'small fry' very often anyway.

CHAPTER THREE: MEMORIES OF FAIRBRIDGE FARM SCHOOL

There was one thousand acres of land that I would get to know. I thought my new home was incredibly awesome. Fairbridge was a picture framed in the wilderness of this place called Canada. The massive Douglas fir trees and the stillness of the forest and unbroken land captivated my mind. I sensed adventure awaited and imagined that I was a pirate in a strange world. I was snapped back to reality as my name was called. I was assigned to a wood cottage that housed 12 to 14 boys. A cottage Mother was in charge and she lived in a suite in the cottage. Her job, I believe, was to keep us towing the line and doing all the cottage chores. The first week or so was spent introducing us new kids to our new surroundings, rules, routines, boundaries, school, the layout of the farm, and – let's not forget – the Anglican Church of England where many hours were spent, even though I was baptized a Catholic. Years later, this would change my whole attitude toward religion.

There were never-ending chores, regardless of your age or size. We slept on steel beds, two sheets and one blanket. The bottom sheet would be washed once a week and the top sheet would now be on the bottom. Fairbridge had its own laundry where the Fairbridge girls toiled. I learned how to make what we called a 'French bed'. This was done by pulling up the bottom sheet and folding it in half. The bed looked perfectly fine until the unsuspecting boy going to bed found out that his feet would only go halfway into bed. The instigators at the time would double up with glee and the cottage mother would come running. She would try to identify the culprit of the prank, but to no avail.

One mean thing the bigger boys would do to me was pin me under a bed cover. I would be on the verge of suffocation, the Hudson's Bay blanket leaving me out of air, red in the face and gasping. This was a real matter of concern so us little ones took care of it by banding together for protection, as it was not right to squeal. Henceforth, we were left alone. I have suffered from claustrophobia since I left the farm. I learned to make a bed and mighty the corners as good as any soldier in boot camp. We were taught how to sew and darn. The limited socks we had would get holes, usually in the heel area. I would use a light bulb, which was available for this chore. By pushing the light bulb inside the sock against the hole, one was able to thread wool horizontally and then vertically till the hole was patched. We were never allowed to sleep in and were up and at it by six in the morning. All kids did the chores assigned to them and after two weeks we would rotate. Beds were always made and you could see your reflection through the wax shine on the floors. A train bell that was donated by the CPR Railroad long before I arrived governed our lives to a large extent. A different number of gongs meant different things, but after all these years I cannot remember them all. One could hear that train bell all over the inhabited area of the farm.

We ate our meals in a huge common dining hall that was quite some distance from the cottages. There were two of us on this detail. We ate out of tin dishes that we had to transport back and forth to the huge dining hall. When the train bell sounded the right number of gongs, we would run as fast as lightening to get in line for food. Some of us being small and young had to stand up together so as not to get bullied out of our place. I still remember my arm around the tin plate protecting some of what we fancied to be a special treat or dessert. After the meal we returned to the cottage, washed and dried the tin dishes and they were ready for the next run. We only ate in the cottage for Sunday breakfast, which consisted of some kind of store-bought cereal. This was a treat!

I must mention that I have not eaten porridge or fatty stew since leaving Fairbridge in 1950.

I adjusted pretty well to life at Fairbridge, just as an inmate adjusts to jail. The big difference was I did not know what crime I had committed and quite frankly, did not know any other way. Not knowing what placed me in this labour-intensive camp was not for me to know, and sadly the truth will never surface. Fairbridge had fields that seemed to go on forever in the eyes of this little boy. Fields had crops and crops had weeds. Little boys got to pull the weeds from the endless rows of the future food supply. If it was not weeding, we piled firewood for the cottage and other buildings after the older boys split cord after cord. This work was usually done on Saturdays after our regular chores were done. There was our own private school which I recalled liking very much. I remember getting a general proficiency award and receiving a book titled "Ticktock and Jim" which I treasured for many years. The book was about the love between a boy and his horse. I read it over and over. I have loved animals forever, especially dogs and horses. Even Wooly, the only dog on the farm had a special bond with me. Today I have a purebred Rottweiler. Her name is Nikita, or Niki for short. As with all animals, Niki gives all her love and devotion the way that only an animal can do.

The town of Duncan was about five or six miles from Fairbridge Farm School. There was the odd time that we went to Duncan unescorted, which was strictly against the rules we were supposed to abide by. The hike into Duncan on the dusty road with one or two of the other boys is a fine memory. We must have looked like Dr. Mengle's children, the 'Boys from Brazil'. We were not cloned, but we dressed the same (if you could call it that). Khaki short pants were everyday dress. We wore no underwear, socks, or shirts in the balmy warm days of summer. We could hear the town's people talk and some obviously whisper about 'those kids from that Orphanage' or Fairbridge. Little did they know, we studied them just as intently. When we did speak, I believe the people loved our English accents but were for the most part, glad to see us head back out of town. If they had only known, we were not Fagan's vagrants, pickpockets, or thieves. Quite the opposite! We were curious and mischievous, but we knew right from wrong.

We were disciplined severely the time we did get caught out of bounds, but it was worth it. One day the school in the town of Duncan had a fire and our private school at Fairbridge was going to accommodate some of the town students until the damage had been assessed and repaired. At first the town kids were weary of our dress, speech, and general well-being. I can only guess they had heard things said about us in their own school and town. However, being kids, we soon got accustomed to each other and they quickly realized we were not freaks, but well-disciplined boys, for the most part. We taught, shared, and let them play English games that they had never heard of. Conkers was a good game. The conker was a chestnut, hopefully baked to take the greenness out of it and to make it hard. A string or shoelace was threaded through the center of the conker and you would hold your conker vertically, suspended by the string or shoelace. Your opponent would take a downward whack with his conker and try to smash yours to smithereens. If he failed to smash your conker then it was your turn, and so on till one of the conkers bust. The winner took on other contenders and added the losing conker points to his winning conker. You could trade winners for new green ones or carry on until yours got smashed.

We also taught them marble games we had learned in England and how to build their own kites out of a simple frame and paper. We watched some of them fly in the wind, way up in the sky. We also showed them how to play soccer the English way, as indeed that was our favorite sport and we played well. They came to realize that we did not have material things like bicycles or store-bought toys or a mum and dad to go home to when the school day was over. For us, work started again after school. I would always look forward to the next day and sharing time with my new friend, Johnny from the Duncan school. There was a distinct difference and curiosity opening up in my mind. The difference between the town kids and us struck fear of the unknown into my young mind. A million questions started to surface but would go unanswered for many years. Somehow, arrangements were made for me to spend a weekend with Johnny and his parents on their family farm. I remember how amazing it was. They lived in a lovely home, which did not resemble my cottage at all. I had never been in such a place that was called 'home', and only three people lived in it. I felt awkward and out of place with all the attention. *Was this affection?* I wondered.

The house had many rooms and beautiful furniture that made my eyes pop. I would look but not touch. Johnny had his own bedroom and things called pillows on the bed. We ended up play fighting with them and got gently scolded by his mum. I tried to go to sleep that night with a pillow, but it was on the floor in the morning. To this day I prefer to sleep without a pillow. When I later inquired about a pillow back at Fairbridge I was told that pillows give you round shoulders, and so be it. Johnny had a mountain of toys and a crystal set you could listen to radio channels on. I got on a bicycle for the first time in my life. After a fall or two I got the hang of it, wobbly as it was. I could not remember ever having a meal, especially home cooked and delicious, in my entire life. To eat all I wanted without fear, and with only four of us at a family table had put me beyond my limits of comprehension. I watched in awe as Johnny's mum talked on a telephone. His mum and dad could not stop laughing. I believe they were starting to understand my tragedy long before I did. Their old farmhouse still stood vacant some distance from the main house. In it was an old wall phone and Johnny's mum said we could talk back and forth from the old house to the new one. We spent endless time and laughter on the phone.

That visit was the start of my quest to try and understand my purpose in life. It hit me hard and fast when I was alone. The empty feeling of reaching for something that was not to be had was difficult for a youngster to handle. I had no questions, as no one would answer if I did. Sometimes, I would wake in the night feeling exhausted from tears and mind overload. There were others around, but the alone feeling was overwhelming. I adjusted back to the world I knew, as the town kids went back to their own school in Duncan. Winter came with lots of snow. Winter chores of snow removal and packing firewood were added to the list of our regular workload. My memory of Johnny and his family was just that – a warm pleasant memory of a time gone by. I was now facing a look at my own destiny, as I knew now at my tender age that something had gone drastically wrong. I decided to try and survive the parts of life that were missing and excel in the good things that I was made of. Then one day it happened! Johnny and his mum and dad were there to take me to their home again. All the caution I had built up in my mind and any negative expectations I had were blown out the window. I was hugged and cooed to and started to feel some emotions and a great feeling of warmth. When we pulled into the long driveway at their farm, I noticed a beautiful black horse running along the fence line, a new addition. I thought of my book *Ticktock and Jim* and had a very pleasant daydream. This horse was nothing like the huge Clydesdale workhorses they used at Fairbridge to plow the fields and perform many other farm duties.

I got settled quickly, as I was not at all shy around this family and was eager to join in. Johnny's dad hooked up the black horse to a cutter (a horse drawn sled) with silver bells and all. Talk about dashing through the snow! This would become one of my finest memories of all time, as so many have disappeared like smoke in the wind. Sadly, that weekend closed the chapter on that part of my life, as I would never see that family again. My mental fortress was getting stronger and I learned not to dwell on things that were out of reach. I wish though, that I had remembered Johnny's last name. Some of the older boys were putting snow sleds together out of barrel staves and anything they (or we) could muster. The sleds were built complete with steering and waxed runners. We were ready and were off to what we called the "chicken house hill'. It was named that because of the proximity to the farm buildings that contained the farms own supply of chickens. I was glad that hill was long and steep. Some sleds would hold six or eight kids that would show no fear. My memory still sees brave kids trying the hill on a single barrel stave, sort of like slalom water skiing! I cannot remember any one of us making that run in one piece. Olympic bob sledding (which I have seen since) has nothing on the rush we felt roaring down the "chicken house hill". I know one thing for certain, those sleds of yesteryear would out race anything bought at a store.

This time at Fairbridge was my life and apart from Johnny's family, was all I knew and had. For the most part, I think we kids got along quite well. The one-thousand-acre farm was ours to conquer, and try we did. The river called Koksilah ran through the farm property. Each year a big bulldozer was brought in and would create a dam with a sluice box to hold the river back. This made a perfect swimming hole where we learned to sink or swim in the coldness of the river water. In you went, bare-assed, one after the other. We spent a lot of time in the river and got to be competent swimmers. When we had time for play or adventure, we would amuse ourselves with no supervision-that I recall. We would try to catch the huge rainbow trout that everyone spoke about with bent pins and string, or whatever we could fashion or borrow. We put a fort together in the deep forest and pretended we were in the world at a different time. The fort was made out of windfall logs, branches, ferns, and what have you. We would try to hide it like a pirate hides his gold. Being young boys, we could be quite mischievous, and I was pretty good with my homemade slingshot. We would hunt for the mighty wasp or hornet's nest and pepper it until it fell from the branch it was hanging from. After stirring up the nest we would run like there was no tomorrow, faster than the wind could blow. Every now and then one of us would pay the piper with a sting or two, but nothing would deter us from this sport. There was a pond situated on the farm in an area called the benchlands. It was laden with frogs and tadpoles. There were a couple of rafts always afloat for our enjoyment. The pond was not clear water like the river, but murky and slimy from little movement. Now and then, someone (including me!) would fall off the raft into this mostly stagnant water, much to the merriment of our chums. In a document I read many years later, the cottage mother's report on me said "the boy has trouble keeping clean".

As I put these thoughts of yesteryear on paper, some fond memories bring a chuckle and warmth as the reel of motion pictures goes through my aging mind. Fairbridge was my home and at the time, I knew nothing different than that institutional way of life. I had no idea the pressure and turmoil that would be placed on me in the near future. In 1948, one of the kids got tonsillitis and had to have his tonsils out. The next thing you know, all of us kids were getting what we referred to as 'laughing gas' and getting our tonsils out (whether we needed to or not). Another time it was ringworm. That time we had our heads shaved and purple colored stuff was painted on our heads. Most other things like chickenpox, mumps, measles, scarlet fever, and whooping cough I already had according to some very old documents. Church was a very big part of our lives at Fairbridge and we attended faithfully every Sunday to worship and put a penny in the collection plate. The chapel was very quaint and very Anglican and is still in use today for various functions. The wooden framed picturesque chapel could seat three hundred people. Trees, peace, and tranquility surrounded it.

Some of the old Fairbridgians meet there every year for a reunion. I returned with my family a few years ago and let my own memories guide me back in time. The sound of singing reached my ears and appeared to echo through the wooden boards of this house of worship. Tears entered my eyes as my heart joined the singing. I believe a man named Tom Hipp was the minister when I was a boy, and he had a son name Peter. My favorite memory of the chapel was harvest time when the fruits of our labour were present. Sunday school was another part our life and it was fully accepted by me. My two daughters had a hard time believing we ate off of tin dishes and that dad went to church, *Wow*! The shock came years later when I found out I was baptized a Roman Catholic and sent to Canada as a Protestant. It would not be long now that cracks would appear in my life story, and I would face a nightmare of cruelty bestowed upon my young soul for the rest of my days.

* * *

A thought just crossed my mind that I had my fifteen minutes of fame at Fairbridge. I starred in the play *Tom Sawyer* live before my peers in the school auditorium. I remember Becky Thatcher and Tom had a problem with strawberry jam that was required in a scene. The jam got all over our faces and the audience howled with laughter. I can't remember who played the part of Becky, but if you're out there... please get in touch. In real time I guess I wasn't at Fairbridge as long as I thought, but to a small boy, just over three years seemed like an eternity. The endless days and starry nights of the nineteen-forties linger in my fond memories of so long ago. Creating dreams as I stared into the heavens, picking out star formations such as the Little Dipper, the Milky Way, wondering about the man on the moon, and how the Mariners learned how to navigate by studying the world above. I still have that fascination for navigation these many years later. Times like that were good. I was fed, clothed, schooled, disciplined, worked hard, and could swear like hell!

I was verbally abused and forever bossed around but I don't remember any sexual abuse against myself. To be perfectly honest, I believe a lot of my young life is blocked out to this day. Unfortunately, there is no human being that can help me with my past. Some of the other kids (now in their adult years) have told me stories of sexual abuse that send shock waves through me. They claim that indeed I was abused and made to perform sexual acts on older boys. Even now at times, my mind will search the past only to shut down any thoughts that strain to surface. Quite simply put, I didn't stand a chance in hell at that tender age of guiding any part of my own life. It was implied that children should be seen but not heard. One of my saddest memories, just every now and then, was wondering why I didn't have a brother or sister like other kids. Something deep inside me told me I did. Time passed and memories of England faded. I went along never trusting my own thoughts to do with any kind of real or imaginary family. I just did not know. The adults at the time, never spoke to me about my childhood in England. The past became extremely dim and I accepted the fact that I was very much alone. I received a document almost sixty years later from the Archives in Liverpool England. It states in cold words, *"it is better to make the Lad forget about his family and life in England."*[1]

I cannot remember ever hearing the word, or receiving a thing called 'love'. Fairbridge was no comparison to the American TV show *The Waltons* that I watched in envy many years later. If only I could have had it that 'tough'.

---

1. Original document scanned and provided on page 147.

Fairbridge beat, or at least tied *The Waltons* in natural geography, but there certainly was not the family atmosphere the Walton family enjoyed. *So much for fiction!* The day came when I noticed that some of the kids were disappearing. I would never I supposed, see them again. The only thing that seemed stable in my life was being taken away.

It was enough to break my heart. *Don't these grown-ups realize the trauma they put us through?* All we had was each other – little friends that had survived a war, crossed the rugged North Atlantic Ocean, crossed a foreign nation, and landed here together. Now we faced total separation. *And we were told there was a 'God'.* My turn came to be looked at and evaluated. Adult people that seemed very nice were checking me out. I was told to speak, and the people got a big kick at my English accent. Some folks tweaked my cheeks and were very pleasant. They left and I thought that was that, and things were back to normal for me. I couldn't have been more wrong.

CHAPTER FOUR: TOMMY LOVICK

I was dressed up real slick one day and driven to Victoria where I boarded a beautiful ship. I have always remembered that steam ship (*Princess Margaritte*), she was sold for scrap in the nineteen nineties. I remember it was dark as we crossed the thirty-eight miles of Pacific Ocean that separated Vancouver Island from the mainland. Miss Christopherson accompanied me. I must admit that lady stuck by me through thick and thin as the time marched by. It turned out she was a social worker with the Children's Aid Society. As I grew, I learned to hate that system with a passion. The voyage on the *Princess Margaritte* was awesome to a kid like me. The dining room was absolutely the most beautiful thing I had ever seen. I was used to tin dishes; one knife, fork, spoon, and a tin plate and cup. Let me tell you, seeing all this was a lot to take in. I had manners from the days of Oliver Twist, the very basics. The silverware alone was hard to comprehend. There were so many knives and forks for just one meal. I can remember steaming under Lions Gate Bridge and looking at all the lights of the harbor and the magnificent splendor of the Hotel Vancouver. Of course, I did not know the names of anything at this time, but to me as a young boy it seemed like a fairy tale.

At this point in time my little world was spinning with excitement, and any thoughts of Fairbridge were on the back burner. We docked in Vancouver and disembarked. I followed Miss Christopherson very obediently, and my mind reeled with excitement. Then it happened. I was being introduced to a man and lady who for the first time in my young life, I would call Mum and Dad. The man smiled and I believe he called me 'son'. The blonde-haired lady was beautiful, and I sensed that I would truly be loved and wanted. I would need to let go of a lot of the coldness and apathy I had built up in myself. Fairbridge, and bits and pieces of the war years continued to flood my young mind. God it was hard, but I knew I belonged to these people and I should try to be on my best behaviour. We got into a shiny red car which the man drove. It was a Packard – a thing of beauty it truly was. As we drove, the lights of the downtown core flew by. I didn't know where I was going and did not care. As long as this was not a dream, I could begin to cope with this new world. The Packard pulled into a driveway, and the engine stopped. You would think I would be tired from all of this, but I was very awake. My eyes must have popped at the sight of the home I was looking at and going to live in. I was introduced to a boy and a girl who would now be my brother and sister. Doug was three years younger than I was and was adopted. The girl, Pat, was three years older. I was eleven. We all hit it off quite well, even though I wasn't a city kid. I have to be honest and tell you, I could swear like a trooper at that age but turning it off and playing 'the angel' was second nature to me. As I said, the house was like something out of a fairy tale.

This was 1950 and there was a television. I did not know what a television was. There was also a huge piano that I would later take lessons on. Looking back, I wish someone had kicked me in the ass and made me follow through with those lessons. There was a swimming pool in the back yard, another mind blower. *Life was beginning to look up for this kid*, I thought as I dove into the pool, much to the horrified look on Mum's face when I surfaced. I suppose she thought I was fragile? Wrong! I didn't even think before I did it. How could Mum know what we did at Fairbridge where we were growing up with little hearts of stone and feelings that were stretched like elastic bands, ready to snap at any time. The tin dishes, the never-ending chores, the strict way of life to be banished forever. God, this had to be heaven. I shall tell you about the live-in maid. Her name was Miss Poshman, a name I shall never forget. I loved her too, she prepared the meals and set the tables and such.

There was a little bell on the dining room table and if you needed her, you rang the little bell. I got severely scolded for ringing that darn bell. I was simply timing Miss Poshman with my new watch to see how fast she could appear. On the other hand, we did share precious moments. I would be up early and down to the kitchen to see her. She would always squeeze the orange juice the natural way, as it was good for my health she said. We became fast friends, but she had to leave because she was getting married. How sad I was. It was rather unusual for me to show emotion. However, all good things have a way of falling apart, and it was about to happen to me. My brand-new world was about to be invaded. I was placed in a school called Vancouver College, an astute Catholic school in its day. "That's all I need" my mind thought, "More bloody discipline and now a strange religion". My heart was broken, but who did I have to tell. Didn't anyone consider my history with my own Church and my own religion? After all that I had witnessed and lived through at such a young age, was I the only one that knew I was a Protestant? All the praying and church during the Second World War and at Fairbridge, plus all the hours spent at Sunday school meant nothing? What was I to do? Rebel, of course. And so, this other saga of my young life began.

When I arrived at the Catholic school my mind was on full alert. I vividly remember sitting in a classroom with a bunch of kids that were all dressed identically. That did not phase me, as I had been there before. A man came in – I remember thinking he looked like a bat – all dressed in black, with his robes flowing as he walked. I was totally unhappy in this environment and raised my hand. The man acknowledged and I asked, "Please sir, may I leave the room?". The man replied,
"You must be Tommy. You will call me 'Father' like the rest of the children". I came back with words of ice,
"You are not my father; he died during the war". I can still see the cold stare he gave me and the bland expression on the other kids faces, along with the look of shock. The silence in the classroom was as though the air quit moving, but I remained defiant. I never went back there and was now to be labeled a 'problem child' for the rest of my young life.

God, it hurt something awful to feel so damn alone. I felt like I was on a roller coaster of emotions and sensed a big change right then and there. *Yes Thomas, you are no longer at Fairbridge with your little British friends, eating and working alongside them.* All of a sudden, a great loneliness came over me and I longed for the people of my own kind. Riches could not erase what I had lived through. I was only eleven years old and my strong religious beliefs had been tampered with three times already. I made up my mind about that time to believe in myself only, and park all that other stuff forever. Fifty years have gone by and the whole world knows what went on with the Christian Brothers of the world and that very school I attended. At least I saved my young body from possible abuse and destruction. Years later I would learn that I did have a brother and sisters who were shipped to Australia and were raised under the Father Rules. There is no way I would dance to their drumbeat.

25

* * *

Tommy Isherwood is now called Tommy Lovick. Life continued with my adoptive parents and I went to a public school named Maple Grove Elementary. I felt better, but I lacked something inside. I had a sense of being wanted and liked, but it was hard to trust. I had an untouched soft spot in my heart but lived defensively and learned to evaluate situations quickly. I was poorly skilled in the cuddles department, but I thought I was getting the hang of it. I guess it did not show but looking back, I cared for and loved those four people more than any of us would ever know. The turbulence seemed to have subsided, and things appeared good for a while. We all took a train trip from Vancouver, British Columbia. I was excited and looked forward to a new adventure.

The stations in all their grandeur and the steam engines were in my life once again. "All aboard," was called and we were on our way to Chicago, a city in the state of Illinois in the United States of America. I still remember the dining car on the train that was absolutely beautiful. I was used to the fancy place settings by now, but there was always something new or unexpected. The waiter put a pretty long-stemmed glass full of scented water and pink things floating around on the table. I could not wait, I raised the glass and chomped what turned out to be a rose petal in a finger bowl. The dark waiter's eyes showed his disbelief, and he must have gone and hid to stop from laughing. I think I was the only one that wasn't uncomfortable. Eventually, we ended up at Lake Simcoe in the Province of Ontario where Ottawa, the capital city of Canada is. Four of us enjoyed a fine holiday at the lake while Dad commuted by car to his office in the city of Toronto (about sixty miles south of Lake Simcoe).

Overall, we got along very well, apart from the pains of my adjustments to a new lifestyle. Barring a vicious lightning storm around the lake area, which appeared to only excite me, the travel was wonderful, and I never ran out of questions to ask. I was indeed inquisitive and absorbed all things new. When I thought the holiday was nearly over, a brand-new Oldsmobile car showed up. We travelled across all the northern states of America, back to beautiful British Columbia, Canada in that car. *What more could a kid ask for?* I cannot remember anything that seemed out of the ordinary after that. I do recall one thing that bugged Mum and that was my inability to keep footwear on, especially rubber boots. It must have been a throwback to the orphanage where barefoot was always in season.

One day I was put in the big red Packard. Mum was driving and she seemed very upset. I had no idea about what and could not believe what happened next. My new world was about to blow up. I still remember the street signs stating Fourth and Alma as the Packard rolled to a halt in some part of Vancouver. I was greeted by someone saying, "Come along Tommy, come along now". For the first time in my life my whole body seemed paralyzed except for the heaving sobbing and tears that ran down my face. I looked at the lady that was my Mummy, she looked devastated and so upset that I cannot describe in words. The Packard roared off as I stood there, still sobbing with no understanding of what was going on.

* * *

A beautiful thing happened many years later when we teamed up again. Mum was going on ninety and we were in touch often. It was late in life, and she was the only woman I ever recognized as my Mum - then, and now. I have remembered Fourth and Alma forever, and still do not know why it happened. There had to be something I wasn't told. Mum said, "It's the worst mistake I ever made, letting you go". All I could say was,
"Yah, tell me about it".

* * *

As I stood watching the Packard drive off, what I did not know then was that my pilgrimage through my young life would have many foster homes and schools yet to chart and I would run the gauntlet over and over again. I decided then that my young life would hear of no more tears and for a while my heart turned to stone. Nothing came in and nothing went out. I was on a journey to become a survivor, happy outside but very sad inside. It still applies to this very day, if I allow myself to slip back in time and revisit those days of yesteryear. Whoever said that the past could come back to haunt you was dead on the money.

Looking back, I think the change was pretty dramatic for the adults and me. My name was now Tommy Lovick and everything I saw or touched was new and exciting. I must have appeared very unpolished to this fine couple but needed some guidance to help me through such a radical change. I would ache inside for attention but did not have the words to convey the hurt inside me. I could not understand how people and religion could flip-flop. All they had to do was ask the child. The simple answer would be that his mind was moving too fast and he was overloaded with this drastic change in his life. Home, school, name change, and religion. Plus, the dramatic change from institutional farm life to one in a fairy tale!

Well, the tears stopped after what seemed to be an eternity. I felt alone, confused, and so heartbroken. It just seemed like I had been granted a family for the first time and all of a sudden, I was placed on the shelf like a broken unwanted toy. *Did this happen in all families? Was I that bad that I had to be thrown to the wolves?*

I made my way into this big old house situated at Fourth and Alma in Vancouver. My eyes were swollen from the streams of endless tears and my mind was searching to understand. The old house sure wasn't like the mansion I had left – no swimming pool, maid service, and most of all, no family. I would not see a television again in a home till 1953. The big old house turned out to be a home for wayward girls, and a brand-new adventure for Tommy. The girls were older than me and immediately took a shining to me, treated me as a little brother. They also showed no concern as to what they would or would not wear in front of this seemingly innocent little chap with the strong English accent. If they had only known then that I was not a spoiled little rich brat. I had not had time to become one. The truth was, I could have held my own in a swearing contest with the best of them, as Fairbridge had taught me well. The girls were very fond of me, and in their own way cared for me ever so much. The feeling became mutual, but deep down there was still a great feeling of loneliness.

I became a young master at controlling fear and emotion. I knew when to please and not to please, and realized I was becoming a genius at perception. This society did not understand the inner workings of a child like me. Very seldom was I asked how I felt or what I would like to do. I was starting to find most adults boring, as most foster homes believed in the now famous words, 'children should be seen and not heard'. Even today my boss has said, "If I had a kid like you, I would have killed you!". The good part is he doesn't mean it! I hope. Well, as a kid (as we all know) time seemed to stand still, but another tomorrow always came.

The girls and I had to part company. I was just put there while they found another home to place me in. I was sad to leave them, but I was already getting the hang of 'no emotional ties'. My young life had prepared me, unknowingly, for what cruelty lay ahead. Miss Christopherson, my Children's Aid worker, picked me up at the home the night before I had to leave and took me to see the movie *Captain Blood* starring Errol Flynn, at the Dunbar movie theatre. "A superb pirate," I thought. I am sure Kay could not wait to get out of there. Kay was an excellent person and would have kept me if she could have.

CHAPTER FIVE: NEWTON

Well, I am old enough to call Miss Christopherson 'Kay', as I write now, so here we go again. I cannot guarantee exact dates, but they should be close.

* * *

It was 1952, and I recall sitting in the car as Kay drove. She wound her way out of the city of Vancouver and eventually drove over the Pattulla Bridge, which spans the mighty Fraser River to connect the Royal City of New Westminster to the young Municipality of Surrey on the south side. As we neared the toll station to pay the twenty-five cents on the Surrey side of the river, something happened. My eyes welled up with tears as the memory of crossing this bridge before entered my mind. I had crossed with 'Mummy' on the way to a holiday at a place called Crescent Beach, on the blue Pacific Coast. There was a flash of how it used to be, now gone forever. I fought the feelings till they all but diminished, but they did not ever disappear completely.

We arrived at an old farmhouse in a place called Newton – talk about the 'green grass of home' – *yikes! I wanted maid service back!* Kay got out and started talking to a couple that lived there, and then she introduced me. There was a kid hanging onto his mother and he said, "Do ya wanna play with my train?" I was not into playing with baby junk, especially a wooden train with wooden wheels. I humored this skinny little kid for a while. He was nine years old and I was going on thirteen. Then, a Collie dog appeared. She looked just like Lassie, but they called her Sally. It seemed like I could bond with most animals quicker than I could with the humankind. Kay had some tea and then it was time for her to leave me there, but she promised she would come back. I did not realize that was part of her job, coming back to see me. I waved good-bye. I had no idea at that point that I had been dubbed a 'problem child'. Nothing could be farther from the truth. The family had a young daughter about five years old that seemed to like me a lot and accepted me as an older brother. They burnt sawdust in the cook stove and wood in the furnace down in the spooky basement where I scared the hell out of their boy now and then.

The man had a little English Thames truck with which he would deliver fresh fish throughout the entire Municipality of Surrey. I would accompany him to New Westminster where he would pick up his product. I recall being quite good at calling out "Fish for sale!", as he would drive slowly through the scattered neighborhoods. I grew to like this man. He was from England and had run a trap line with his friend in Alberta. The man's name was Leonard but he was only called that when his wife Mona, was cheesed off at him, which was often! He knew about carpentry, as he had apprenticed for that trade. Len was reasonable. Mona was hard to please, as time would prove. It turns out they divorced thirty-six years later. Hell, nobody is perfect. I inherited the chores when Mona figured I had adjusted. There would always be sawdust to haul in for the cook stove, which was designed to supply the hot water. I hauled the sawdust from an old shed fifty feet from the house in five-gallon buckets. The wood and coal for the basement furnace was another frustrating job. The stairs and the low door leading to the basement always made it a challenge. Doing the dishes was a job I was good at, but not one I liked. Their little boy Billy was too young and small to do chores, so the responsibility lay with me. The difference was always there, and didn't I know it. I attended school in Whistle Stop, in the small town of Newton.

The town consisted of a few stores and a couple of gas stations. If you sneezed driving by you would miss it. I rode my bicycle to school, about eight miles round trip. I was appointed the first Highway Crossing Guard at the school. I could stop traffic on the King George Highway to let my friends cross safely. Man, did I feel important when I put my official hat and safety vest on! One day after school I noticed one of my bike tires were low on air. I made it to the Texaco gas station where the attendant knew me. I was busy putting air in the tire when I heard the yipping of puppies coming from inside the service station. My love for dogs caused me to investigate and I followed the sound inside. There was not one, but nine little Labrador puppies all striving for my attention. I picked each one up and they fidgeted and licked my face. I asked if I could have a pup and the Guy said, "Kid, ya can have all of them". Wow! You should have seen Mona's face when I arrived with nine little pups in my paper carrier. Fortunately, Mona also had a soft spot for dogs, and I knew this. We found new homes for eight and kept one. At this point in time, Mona had fifteen dogs and close to a dozen kids running around the five-acre farm. Mona ran us like a two-bit business and really failed to have a grip on things. I was the cheeky one, and she certainly seemed to enjoy threatening me a lot of the time.

Mona made all the decisions and I used to wonder why Leonard did not stand up to her. One day, Mona decided to pile all the kids except me into the van and drive to the town of Cloverdale to take in the fall fair. I was doing my 'Huck Finn' activities outside as darkness fell, and they were all inside the house getting dressed for the fair. At that moment I decided that if I couldn't go, nobody would go. I let the air out of all the van tires, including the spare. Nobody went to the fair. I remember how Mona was mad, the kids were sad, but I was extremely glad. I figured that Mona was a user of the Children's Aid Society, and time would prove me right. My days here were numbered, but it did not phase me at all. Mona was a clone of Fagan (the fictional character in Charles Dickens' novel, *Oliver Twist*). Life went on at the five-acre farm and another foster child arrived. Her name was Sandra, and she was just a baby. In his spare time, Len was remodeling the old house. I helped him as much as I could. Mona started getting on my case a lot and the rebellious side of me surfaced. I would not allow myself to get pounded on physically or emotionally, not ever again. If things did not please her, she would threaten to call Kay to come and pick me up. I would reply, "Go ahead."

My life was turning miserable and I could not stand that bitch. Nothing I did would please her. I would spend a lot of time with Len who had a new job delivering parcels. I saved him a ton of legwork running the parcels up long country driveways, making change for C.O.D., and fending off a variety of animals. The animals didn't all like me and I was chased more than once. Len's truck had a sliding door on the passenger side. Once on foggy day, and as he turned a corner the door slid open and I fell out into the fog. Len and the truck disappeared instantly. I was okay and quickly got off the roadway. It seemed like a lot of time passed, but then I made out the shadow of the truck going very slow. The side door was still open, and I bailed in. Len was laughing hard and I could not help but join in. A few scrapes and bruises were no big deal. Len had installed the latest linoleum in the kitchen for Mona, the kind that just required liquid wax. One day, Mona was having tea with her friend and neighbor Vie, in the sunroom just off the kitchen. Mona had just given the floor the Johnson Wax treatment. Both women were enjoying the new product when I arrived at the door with my full pails of sawdust for the stove. I had no idea about the floor being waxed, and as I opened the door and noticed the high sheen that the wax had created, I stopped short.

No damage was done, but at that very instant Mona chose to call me names in front of her friend that I shall not repeat. I threw the contents of both buckets over her stinking shiny floor. It seemed that the wax and sawdust were not compatible. My punishment later was to be locked up in a bedroom on the third floor of the farmhouse. As soon as darkness arrived, I was gone out the window using blankets and sheets tied together. They were a little short and I hit the ground like a ton of bricks. Being a ward of the government had some advantages, if you knew what to do. I had somebody phone Kay Christopherson, and I was on my way again.

CHAPTER SIX: BOYS' HOME

Well, I had done it this time. I was sent to a boys' home for problem children situated in the West End of Vancouver. I guess Mona did not give me a good report. There were twelve boys in this home, and they were not at all ready to take home to meet your mother. Twelve boys and twelve different stories to be told, each one unique and sad. My Fairbridge skills would prove to be extremely valuable here. Like a grizzly bear, I had to mark my territory and was soon accepted. This was no place for wimps or the faint of heart. There were exceptions of extreme dysfunction, like the kid that tried to separate my head from my body with a hatchet. I had been working on my bicycle in the basement of the home. I was concentrating on adjusting the chain and was in a crouched position when there was a 'thud' sound above my head and a laugh that was frightening. A hatchet was half buried in the wooden wall stud. I had no time to be frightened and my reaction was instant. I quickly forced his hand into the bicycle chain and turned the pedal to jam his hand so he could not move. Staff, alerted by the noise of me swearing, came to the rescue and witnessed the crazy boy with his eyes still rolling. I believe he ended up in a mental facility and I never saw him again.

Then there was Benny, the boy that Johnny used to pick on. Benny had a glass eye and was visually impaired. By this time, I basically ran the troops and would stand by the weak if they were in the right. Johnny was always running a tad late for supper and one particular night he had Benny upset again. I had Benny remove his glass eye and I quickly put it in the middle of Johnny's mashed potatoes. The look in Johnny's eyes when his fork made contact with the glass eye looking at him was priceless. He left the table with the look of death on his face. We howled with laughter. Believe it or not, Johnny and I became fast friends after that, and he treated Benny just fine. We used Benny's visual impaired card to ride the buses and get into the theatres. Benny could see the movie from the front row. If a few of us decided on a movie, one would get in using the card, and then proceed to open one of the exit doors to let the rest into the theatre. Worked every-time to my knowledge.

Making school lunches was another problem. It was a total waste of time because you never knew if the sandwiches were spit in. They got fired in the garbage, day after day. I relied on my paper route money and other means to fill the nutritional void. Overall, we all got along pretty well. If the going got tough, we would stick together. One day we were told an RCMP officer was going to 'hold the fort' for a weekend. When he arrived, he gathered us together and gave us his version of the rules. Innocently, we gave him the notion that he was completely understood. We did not like his threats or his style, so we made a simple plan to get him in shit! All of us would run away that very night. We would go in pairs. Billy and I teamed up and planned to go to the Caribou country of British Columbia, to get lost and become cowboys.

We made it out of Vancouver to the municipality of Burnaby. Can you imagine our glee when we saw this sleek car idling while the owner was in a phone booth yacking away? I slid behind the wheel of the black beauty and could just barely reach the pedals. I could see through the steering wheel along the very long hood. The dang thing had hydrostatic transmission, no gears to learn. We were on our way in style! We made it out of Burnaby, through New Westminster, and on to that Pattulla Bridge that I had crossed many times with Len to pick up the fish or parcels. I had a quarter ready for the bridge toll. I slowed down to stop but the guy's eyes went big as saucers when he saw me driving, so I hit the accelerator and we were gone. I knew where I was but so did the police, and in no time, I was pulled over with a gun pointed my way and the words, "It's only a kid". I didn't know where the Caribou was anyway. Billy and I had made a pact to tell them nothing, even though they treated us extremely well behind the bars. Back then, of course, they did not have the technology of today. Besides, we were not out to hurt anyone. Try telling that to the guy that came to collect his car and to see if he could identify us. He wanted to beat us up really bad. Anyway, we were transferred to a Burnaby Fire Hall that had a thing that looked like the jail cell we had just left. A big fireman was put in charge of us and he said, "There will be no fooling around, you kids". I asked him if I could have a whiz and he allowed me out, as the biffy was close by. In that second or two I was down that brass pole and running down the street. It turned out Billy went down the other pole as I distracted the burly fireman. Our speed on foot was too much for the guy and he soon gave up. However, we were soon back in custody and returned to the home the next day. We never saw that RCMP fella again. With all the new knowledge I had picked up in the boys' home, and on the streets of the City of Vancouver, I decided this government knew nothing about kids like me. Now they had made me street smart too! – skills I would need later. My time had come to move on to a new adventure. It seems like the government had received a call from Mona. Can you believe *she was asking for me back?* I must have had a huge price on my head, but that move never did happen.

CHAPTER SEVEN: TAP DANCING

This is another part of my life that is truly amazing. I left the Boys' Home to live with one of the kindest ladies that I had ever met. Her name was Ethel, and she had a daughter named Barbara. We got along famously. I was not meant to stay there for a long time, but it seemed like an eternity. I don't remember anyone being sad. I had another new school, a paper route, and I delivered fish and chips a couple of evenings a week. I was settled in and felt wanted. The house was in Vancouver across town from the Girls' Home and all those fond memories I so cherished. I attended Gladstone Junior High School, which was modern compared to Kitsilano Junior that I attended when I stayed at the Boys' Home. Ethel made excellent lunches for me. You see, at the Boys' Home you had chores that you rotated every two weeks, two boys would be on "make the lunch" detail, and we were all famous for spitting in the sandwich of particular individuals. You never knew for sure if they had been switched around unless you made your own. In my world at that time, you had to try to be one step ahead and try to foresee what lay ahead on the trail. These little skills accumulated over time and became invaluable to my well-being.

I never seemed to have a problem making new friends and I was never shy about changing schools. I loved sports and had no problem making some of the school teams such as soccer, softball, and track and field. Ethel would take Barbara and I to Nat Bailey Stadium to watch Pro-ball. The stadium still exists today (in the year 2000). We would go to a place called Sea Island where Ethel's sister and family lived. Her sister's name was Marge (at least she was called that name, to my memory). Marge ran a school called Marge Berry's School of Dance. Marge taught Barbara and other kids tap dancing. I was convinced to try out. I thought, "My God, what if this should leak out, could I stand the ribbing?!" Oh well, I got in line with six girls and one other boy (who I swore to secrecy). The record player was turned on and the words to *Every Little Breeze Seems to Whisper Louise* sung by the Frenchman, Maurice Chevalier played. It was a catchy tune and Marge was teaching '*Toe, Heel, Step*' verbally and physically. The girls were good. Barbara was a natural and the two of us could practice off-site, but she left me far in the dust. The other boy and I gave it up, although secretly I had enjoyed the experience. I enjoyed going for those visits to Sea Island for another reason - It was the home of Vancouver International Airport. I would spend many pleasant hours watching aircraft of all sizes land and take off. There were no commercial jet aircrafts then, but many years later I would fly in and out of Vancouver fairly often, for a time.

The Pacific National Exhibition (PNE) was on and it turned out some of Ethel's relatives followed the Fairs and Carnivals and that's how they made their living. The man's name was Stan, and the boy's name was Jerry. We all got along well. Marge Berry had a group perform on stage at the PNE. Barbara was in that tap dancing group and they were flawless. For some reason it was time for me to move on and leave another nice family behind. I packed up the electric train set I had acquired from paper route money and wondered, "Where to next"? *Doesn't anyone in this world want me?* Little did I know this city would be out of my life for a while. Now that I am in my adult years, I wonder if maybe Barbara's mom and family were concerned about her and I. We had become very close and were in an awkward age group that could have troubled them. We did spend a fair amount of time alone. I read in a local newspaper in 1999 that Barbara had become a celebrity and a star on the television series, *Peyton Place*. I read that her Mum had passed on, and I felt sad as it triggered my mind back to those happy days we shared together.

CHAPTER EIGHT: THE SKELTON'S

Well, this had to set some kind of foster home record. I was taken to live with another family. As Kay introduced me to this couple, I noticed a boy about my age sticking his tongue out, and a snot-nosed girl, who must have been his sister, gawking at me. I had very bad vibes telling me to take a hike. As Kay was still conversing with the couple, I motored out the back door and never looked back. I never learned their names in that few moments before fleeing. This home finding was now becoming a pain in my ass! I think I was now about 13 years old, and in some ways, felt that I had lived a lifetime. I got a hold of Kay much later. I was still in Vancouver, a place I could survive quite well as I knew the area very well.

Kay asked if I would like to live on a farm out in the country where there were animals, and I could have a dog again. That did it for me. "When do I leave", I asked. "Today", was the reply. I had no idea of the hell I was getting into but believe me, it was another adventure. I must have had a high price on my head for people wanting to take me in. I learned later on that the pay was good for fostering problem children. We drove out to a suburb, about thirty miles east of Vancouver. It was called the Municipality of Maple Ridge, and my destination was a Township named Pitt Meadows. The car turned off the road into a big farmyard. My young eyes rapidly scanned and gave the area a quick evaluation. There was an old, well-maintained farmhouse to my left. It had a separate, beautifully maintained yard surrounding it. To my right there was an old barn which appeared to be leaning slightly, but it looked solid. Straight ahead was the implement shed with different types of farm machinery filling the bays. I clearly recognized some of the implements from my time at Fairbridge Farm School, even though I had been much too young to operate them. Little did I know, I would become a young expert in the matter of dairy farming.

Kay and I were greeted by an older couple who appeared to be very warm towards me, and my first impression of them was quite favorable. After about an hour went by and Kay said good-bye to me. I sensed something in her voice and body language that was upsetting me inside. I could not figure it out, but I believe Kay knew that we might never see each other again. She was correct, yet had told me nothing.

39

Even though I had run her around the bend more than once as my Social Worker, we had developed a special bond. I was the boy who could drive her crazy. I will never forget her, especially the way she was after we had watched the movie, *Captain Blood*. Now I was on this farm having to start building a life all over again. Mr. and Mrs. Skelton had four children – two boys and two girls. One girl was named Joan and was still living at home. She was older than me by several years, but we got along well. Her sister Pam and brother Gordon had left home prior to my arriving. The other son Alec and his wife Pat lived in a little run-down shack on the farm, but well away from the main farmhouse. Alec was eleven years older than I was and he ran the farm for his father.

Mr. Skelton commuted to Vancouver where he worked in the office of a large wholesale produce company. I believe the name of the company was Snowboy. I maintained the yard around the farmhouse. This was easy. The work did not frighten me and they treated me fairly well. Alec and I were like brothers at the time. He worked my ass off and taught me a lot. He taught me how to milk cows, separate the cream, clean the barn, know when silage was ready, mow the hay fields and get it to the barn. I could run farm machinery as good as most men. When Alec and I would wrestle in the hayloft, I would make him say 'uncle', as I got the best of him quite often. On top of life on the farm, I went to school on the bus. As mentioned early and still true, school was good for me, and I so enjoyed playing the team sports. Other farmers every now and then would phone to see if I would do some custom work for them. I usually accepted and had no time left, except for school and farm work.

* * *

I could never figure out exactly what happened, but somehow, I was assigned a new social worker. His name was Bruce, and he was not a bad guy. By that time, I had met Alec's in-laws – Pat's parents, Eddy and Millie Gray, her sister Arlene, brother Craig and his wife Donna. I ended up living with Eddy and Millie on their farm a few miles away from Alec and Pat. I started to wonder if people were using me to do the work that was undesirable for them to do. I was treated good but had a feeling of being passed around like a stack of pancakes from one farm to another. I paused at this moment to wonder why. One day, I got the idea to phone Arlene (Pat's sister). She had been living in Vernon, in the interior of BC. Telephone information gave me her phone number.

When I called, Arlene and I chatted away, just like it was yesterday. She was retired after teaching school for thirty-five years. She was a little older but sounded sharp as a tack. She told me that the senior Skeltons had wanted to move back to the city and indeed had done just that. That left me between a rock and a hard place, as the agreement with Eddy and Millie was only for the summer. I became quite sad as I had become fond of them and did not want to go back to the city. The Gray family came to the rescue and for now at least, I would stay with them. I could still be around Craig and Alec, and the farm work still went on. Craig and I ran the dykes that controlled the Allouette River which flowed into Pitt Lake. Craig was in training for a boxing match, and the running kept us both in shape. We enjoyed diving off the silver bridge and swimming in the river that joined their property.

* * *

The day came when I had eyes for a girl at school. It turned out her folks had an eighty-acre farm just a couple of miles from the Gray farm. I started spending most of my time at her parents' farm. They had a milking herd of about thirty-two cows at the time, which was a good herd back then. I started helping with all the farm chores, for free. I was hooked and seemed powerless to change things. I was fourteen years old and 'topsy turvy' in love. I ended up living there. The girl's nickname was Butch, and she had two brothers, Gary and Rick. Butch, Gary, and I would be in the barn around five o'clock every morning to milk the herd. We fed them their food and portion of molasses, then hauled the milk in pails to the milking parlor to run it through the cream separator. We would have the full heavy cans of milk on the milk stand by the road so the truck wouldn't pass them by on its way into town. This left little time to get clean and ready for school, let alone grab some cereal. Usually, we barely made the bus but our youth would persevere. I rarely saw Butch's old man in the barn in those early mornings. He was usually sleeping when we left for school. Guess he had trust in us, but he was short on praise. After school we would clean the barn and do the milking and chores all over again. It sure wasn't a house full of love (which I did not expect) but *God, their own kids?* The friendship between Butch and I became much more than that. It was a bond that could have lasted a lifetime in our young minds. I guess it became noticeable, and soon people were trying to drive wedges between us. A drifter appeared on the farm to do odd jobs. He was an older guy, maybe in his forties, and he developed eyes for Butch. She became frightened. I was

The Best I Remember – A Cruel British Tragedy

fourteen, and felt no fear, so I asked the guy what he was all about. He told me in no uncertain terms to get lost, and the pushing started. The fight was on, and the old guy was amazed at the strength I displayed. Well, that was the end of his days on that farm and shortly after, the end of mine. In a way it was a blessing; never did a boy work so hard to get so little! My life felt full of problems again, and I suffered a great emotional set back. I still saw Butch, but at our young age, things were extremely difficult to figure out. Our dream was to spend a lifetime together, but it was not meant to be.

* * *

Somewhere in between taking the bus to school, an old farmer that I helped out when he needed, got in touch with me. While at his farm he said, "do you know what's under the tarp in the implement shed". I replied, a car, as I had peeked long before out of curiosity. He said, "well son, that car is for you as being visually sight impaired, I can't drive on the roads anymore". My first and very own car, the 1934 Ford coupe was a gift I treasured.

Butch and I quit taking the bus to school, sometimes I would drop her off and then buzz around the school. One day I came around on the road that passed the principal's entrance, low and behold, the tall Vice Principal was standing in the middle of the road waving like crazy for me to stop. No way I thought, I veered over the manicured lawn, through the flowery garden area, never looking back. Later I had a visit from the Haney police who all knew me and had me promise to not drive without a license and to apologize to the Vice Principal. I pointed out that the police had seen me many times driving tractors and farm trucks often on the local roads when doing custom work. However, my promise was good for some time. Winter came, and the freezing weather put my car engine out of business. So back to the bus for a while. All seemed to be forgiven and life went on until Bob the school Superintendent got me a 1949 Lassalle sedan for $10 from a UBC Professor friend and my promise took the back burner.

CHAPTER NINE: THE MARSHALL'S

What I did not know at the time, was that my free labour for certain farmers was over. I don't know for sure how things were worked out with the Child Welfare Branch and Bruce, my social worker, but something pleasant was going to happen! I was placed in a boarding home managed by Mr. and Mrs. Guy Marshall. There were a couple of older men who boarded at the Marshall's. I still remember their names, Eric and Helmut. My assumption was that they were Germans, and I wondered what the hell they were doing here. When I met them, memories and pictures of the war flashed in my mind, and I didn't know whether to like them or not.

* * *

As I slowly get my thoughts on paper, I should point out that today is November 11, 2000. I will stop for now as I have to go to my Branch #265 of the Royal Canadian Legion to pay my own respects to those that lost their lives so others could live in freedom. My wife, Sheryl, has been a member of the Ladies Auxiliary Branch #265 for close to thirty years. Sheryl is a Past President and was awarded her lifetime membership for her outstanding dedication to her branch. My wife left very early this morning to meet up with the other dedicated ladies who will staff the kitchen, as they have done for so many years. Yes, I think of the War. Born in Birmingham, England December 23, 1938, in a house that happened to be in the flight path of the Birmingham Airport. You might say the War Zones became my home. I did not know any other way. When bombs would find their target, or miss and find us instead, I would not dwell on it. I endured every single day of the War, being bombed out, living in the homes for the so called 'under privileged' children, and I was barely six years old. There is never a mention of kids like me in Britain's national history, who have seen so much war. We did not receive any medals. Instead, we were shipped and herded like animals to Canada in 1947, to another home for the 'under privileged'. They say, 'War is Hell', but for some of us, it is never really over. England made sure of that when they brutally separated so many families.

* * *

Mrs. Marshall treated me well and I would go out of my way to please her. She had never had such a young boarder and seemed quite pleased to cater to me. The two German guys seemed all right, but I slept with my door locked just the same. It was so different to be able to do only what pleased me. I had time on my hands, which meant more time at school and playing sports. On weekends, I did a fair amount of custom work for the farmers I had gotten to know. There was a Dutch firm developing land they had acquired for a settlement not far from the Gray's farm. The Dutch called the settlement Pitt-Polder. A superintendent named Chris was hiring local kids for weekend work, from general labor to running loaders and bulldozers. I could run a small bulldozer, so it wasn't too long before I was running one of the big ones – a D9 Caterpillar. After a while I could operate the huge machine quite well, back filling and leveling the land became routine, old hat. Summer holidays were approaching, and I heard the Canadian Pacific Railway (CPR) was hiring people to install more rail yard track in their Port Coquitlam Rail Yard.

Work was supposed to last all summer at one dollar and sixteen cents per hour. *That was for me!* I applied and was hired. The line crew seemed to be made up of mostly Italians and was called a 'section gang'. The job consisted of hard work, creating a new rail bed, hauling rail ties and steel track, aligning the track under the watchful eye of Fred Franson – his lean wiry body with a face that looked like leather. He appeared to be as old as the railroad. I was now sixteen years old and I was to learn a lot from Mr. Franson. That summer of 1955 was quite hot, and my first job was to pack water to the section gang crew, most of who could not speak English. I found it boring and asked Mr. Franson if I could change jobs. The other reason was that he favored me, and it was noticeable to the section gang and the three other kids that worked on the job. I ended up trading with another kid, who soon found out that packing two barrels of water supported around your shoulders was no easy feat either. It wasn't long before he wanted to trade back. The job I had traded for was unloading creosote rail ties out of a boxcar. This job was tough but had far more breaks than packing water. I became so tanned that summer and my belly was so black from the creosote I could have lived on another continent.

I asked Fred (I could call him that now), if I could try pounding spikes with the Italians. A wry grin came over his creased face and he said, "Come on then, I'll make a railroader out of you yet." The Italian crew boss handed me a nine-pound sledgehammer, as the rest of them howled with glee. He could speak English, but everything he said was in Italian. I requested he go first, and he obliged. He tapped his spike to start it into the tie and then with three over-the-head swings he drove the spike home. It didn't look like a big deal to me, I was handed a spike as the whole crew moved out of the way. Fred was grinning along with them. I tapped my spike with no problem, and then the nine pounder was up and over my head in a beautiful ark. I did not spare the horses; I gave it all I had. The head of the sledge caught the top of the new steel rail and I thought I was on the way to the moon. My whole body was ringing, and the whole damn crew was laughing so hard, I started laughing with them. You have to hit those damn spikes just under the lip of the rail or you are going to find out where the saying 'shiver my timbers' comes from! I stayed with that crew for a while and with their patience, I became quite adept at pounding spikes for the railroad. It came in handy when I pounded the pad for ringing the bell at many fairs that I would attend later on in life.

It was hard to believe that I was earning two hundred and sixty-five dollars a month. I was saving feverishly for a car, even though I was only fifteen years old. Things were going good for me during this time. I liked where I lived, the railroad work, Mr. Franson (Fred), and a certain girl, Butch, who was still in my life. The end of summer was approaching quickly. There was less than two weeks of work and then back to school. The work on the railroad and the custom work on the farms, had put me in perfect physical condition. Fred called me aside one morning and told me how pleased he was with my work performance. He heard something about my background from another employee who lived in the neighbourhood and he seemed quite keen on hearing what happened with my young life. I filled him in a little, and he just shook his head in disbelief. Fred said "Kid, I can help you become a fine railroader." Just then there was the familiar sound of a locomotive whistle, Fred reached for his pocket watch as I had seen him do many times before. With a glance he remarked, "Ninety-Nine right on time." The black beauty was strutting her stuff on the mainline. Winding her way East to conquer the Rocky Mountain Range and show all of its splendor to the lucky passengers on board. The plumes of black and white smoke billowed and swirled well above the passenger cars. The big driving wheels with their white sidewalls appeared to pull that train along with little effort. We listened to the familiar *sound clickety clack, clickety clack*, as steel met steel, and the beautiful sound of the whistle as Ninety-Nine disappeared out of sight. We got back to things at hand and Fred carried on where he had left off.

Fred had made arrangements for me to work for the Canadian Pacific Railway on weekends and holidays, so I could continue to attend school. "It's a done deal" Fred said, if that's what I wanted. No more section gang work or packing water. I would be trained in the ways of the railroad and one day become an engineer. We headed toward this enormous building; I already knew it was called the roundhouse, but I had never been inside. It was made of red bricks and was truly round. It was home to the locomotives that needed servicing or repair. Fred introduced me to a couple of guys, then said, "I'll be in touch, Kid." And disappeared. At that moment I felt lonely.

These final days of summer were spent paying a lot of attention to my new job. Plus, I didn't want to let Fred down. The crew at the roundhouse accepted me for my ability to learn and help them out when required. The job I was trained for was called a *Wiper*, which consisted of firing up the huge boiler to make the steam that made these huge machines move. I felt smaller than a peanut in the cab of the engine with the maze of valves and levers. We started with what was called *waste*, that looked like stuffing out of an old chair. I called it kindling. The waste would be soaked in oil and ignited; the boiler was oil-fired, which was fed through atomizers that controlled the flow of oil. The water would pass through the tubes in the boiler. The water flow was controlled by injectors. You had to stay alert and keep your eyes on many gauges; the heat could be excruciating. When the working pressure was reached, you had to maintain it. The older guys told me stories about engines and roundhouses blowing up to smithereens because of carelessness. One story was about "the kid that let off steam before it hit the red line", which I thought applied to life in general.

* * *

Well, I had learned to fire up a steam locomotive on my own, and it was now time to learn how to move them back and forth. There was a thing called the turntable that actually turned and could make a perfect match with the track in the roundhouse or the yard track. The table turned three hundred and sixty degrees. I just loved this part of the work; I got to move these huge Engines out of the roundhouse onto the turntable and down the service track. This track was where the supply depot was located. It contained the fuel, oil, water, and sand that was necessary to operate these giants. Sometimes when I thought no one was looking, I would make the big wheels chatter, steel on steel. This was accomplished by opening the hand throttle wide and then slacking off the throttle. I was doing this mischief one day and I looked down from the cab into Fred's face. He wasn't smiling. I stopped the shenanigans and Fred came aboard and gave me a hard lecture, which I deserved. He asked if I had noticed the new yard engines. "They are powered by diesel fuel", he said, "but they will never replace steam". Well, Fred was wrong, as we all know now.

Times were changing quickly. The diesels were responsible for ending my short career as a railroader. The regular guys were now scrambling for work, so my railroading days (other than being a passenger) were gone forever. A short time later, I heard Fred had passed away. I took a moment to reflect, and never looked back. I truly missed the sauna that Mrs. Marshall had ready for me every day I worked for the railroad. Yes! She was good to me, and so were the two Germans, Eric and Helmut. School was good and I went back to working part-time for different farmers. Something however, was in the wind. Bruce wanted to see me in his office. Our conversation turned sour. Bruce had let the Children's Aid Society in Victoria know that I had been working the summer for the C.P. Railroad. He let them know because he was proud of what I had accomplished and meant no harm to me. Even though I was back in school, they wanted me to pay my own room and board now. I was sixteen years old and balked at this revolting suggestion. There was still no way I could speak for myself, and it was damned frustrating that everything was decided for me by people that did not even know me. I was some pissed off, and retaliated verbally, explaining that many of my friends had worked various jobs and were back at school. They got to keep their money. Also, their parents were kicking in money to help buy them a car as added incentive for getting experience in the work force. I could not believe what they were asking of me, and I decided, "to hell with them!". Foster families were paid to have me in their home, and in turn, I worked hard for them. It seems ironic that the Child Welfare Division would have me pay for the pleasure of working like a hired hand for these people.

* * *

Over fifty years later, I still see how the Ministry operates and read about their many screwups, which confirm in my mind that they do not understand the reality of kids like me. They are too concerned with getting diplomas and do not seek or value experience in the real world.

CHAPTER TEN: BOB

Well, all is not lost, but my memory is a little dull at the moment. For some reason, in late fall of 1955 I recall meeting with Bruce, my social worker, and a man named Bob. Bob and I hit it off right away. He wondered if I would like to stay with his family for a while. My first thought was "Why?". Anyway, I liked him, and decided to have a go. After all, I could bugger off at any time. They owned a small hobby farm in a place called Whonnock, about six miles east of Haney where I still attended school. Bob was the secretary of the entire School District. This blew a lot of minds at school when the kids found out. The little farm was very picturesque, and even supported one milk cow. I would help him with the mediocre chores. Bob owned a 1950 Ford two door automobile – the kind of car you would die for back then. I helped install a continental kit that housed the spare tire and extended the cars length by two feet. We added fender skirts over the rear wheels and *presto!* – it was a car to behold.

I was at the age when I thought life can be full of many surprises, some good, some bad. Shortly after passing my driver's test and being legal to drive, Bob told me he had a surprise for me. Bob had acquired an older vehicle for me and my heart melted when my eyes made contact with my future jalopy. Bob had bought an old 1939 LaSalle sedan for a measly ten dollars from a friend of his I never got to know. I was advised that the LaSalle had a starter problem but fired up quickly by using the hand crank, other than that, it was mechanically sound. The car was a monster compared to my first car, the 1934 Ford coup. The LaSalle had four doors, running boards, and a very long hood. The mass of steel was something my friends had never seen, and in fact many school chums found my prize on wheels quite ugly. Seemed like every kid in school wanted to have a ride.

Usually after school, far from the eyes of the Vice Principal, Teachers, Parents, and Police, we would head to our favorite hill with the LaSalle interior and running boards with kids hanging on. The old car sped down the hill that had a strange up and down feeling in the stomach, similar to one when riding a roller coaster. There was never any thought that what we did was dangerous, and not one of us got hurt. The old LaSalle was in need of a paint job, so friends got together and gave it one in a secret place. We agreed to use paint of many colors and paint to hearts content. The car now looked worse than ever as words like shah-boom, hot dog, Elvis is King, and made a real mess when colors ran into one another.

Things were okay, but I found myself missing Mrs. Marshall. I would visit her quite often and she made quite a fuss over me. When I left it was sad. School was going good. My Saturday job at the Whonnock sawmill setting blocks and learning to operate a forklift paid union rate. The odd time the railroad would call me in as a spare. There was no shortage of work in those days. December came and Bob said he had a surprise. The arrangements had finally been made for me to take my written and road test for my driver's license. I was jubilant. Bob said I could use his car. I guess he didn't want the examiner being a passenger in my little unlicensed 1939 LaSalle. I had no fear, as I knew the test book pretty well off by heart and felt I'd driven a lifetime already. Bob drove east to the town of Mission, which should have been called the town of one thousand hills. I passed the written with no problem. Bob gave me 'thumbs up' and the road test was on. It too, was a piece of cake. After all, I had driven these roads and hills before. The examiner wanted to know where I had acquired such a good command of the automobile. I certainly didn't tell him I had been on the road for over a year in my own jalopy. We shook hands and he said my license would come in the mail, and in the meantime, I should use the interim paper that he gave me. Bob said, "take me home", and the rest is history. I got to use the Ford quite often and I never broke the man's trust in me. To this day I have no idea why I went there, but it turned out alright. Well, life was going along pretty well in 1956.

I was in my final year of high school, participating in sports, and my grades weren't that bad either. I was driving my new jalopy, the LaSalle, legally. What more could a guy ask for? Butch and I were still very close and saw each other often. I felt sorry for her as it had been easy for me to escape the wrath of her parent's farm, not so much for her. I would almost pray for time to move quickly so we could be together forever. It was always an uphill battle, between the adults and us. They knew I came from nowhere and I had no one, so they drove the wedge whenever they could. Even Bruce hinted about our young age. He would preach, "wait and see what the future would bring". Bruce even told the folks in Victoria about our devotion to each other. They called it puppy love and suggested it was a passing fancy. That summer I worked part time with the railroad, doing farm work and working at the lumber mill if needed. I started to think more about the future. The railroad was changing and I sure as hell wasn't going to be a mill worker, and I didn't want to be a farmer. I thought of increasing my education and one day found myself reading a brochure about life in the Canadian Military. I talked to Butch and we decided that would be our future. Separating would be tough, but in the long run, a benefit for the both of us.

CHAPTER ELEVEN: ROYAL CANADIAN AIR FORCE

I told Bruce of my plan to join the military. I expected he would have no objections; except he would have to let the powers that be known. I decided to join the Royal Canadian Air Force, and shortly after was being tested mentally and physically at their Vancouver recruiting facility. My government guardian had to fill out consent forms because of my young age and come up with a birth certificate. Somehow, they came up with that in record time. I felt like they were putting me on the train before it left the station. Lucky for them, I was accepted and would leave Vancouver for the Province of Quebec for basic training in December (which was now only two weeks away). The only one I would truly miss – you can guess – did not show up to say good-bye. The next thing I heard was "All aboard!". It was the passenger train called The Canadian, pulled by a steam locomotive. There was no finer train in Canada. Soon the train would pass the roundhouse and rail yard where I had spent some quality work time.

I listened to the whistle and the rickety rack clickity-clack of steel against steel one more time. I thought of Fred and wondered what lay in wait for me at the end of the line. Man was I ever on my own this time. The Dome car allowed for a spectacular view as we wound our way through tunnels, passes, waterfalls, and snow-capped peaks of the Rocky Mountain range. On more than one occasion I saw different animals such as Moose, Elk, Bear, and Mountain Goats in their own habitat. It was breathtaking and it's difficult to find words to describe the wonders of the Rocky Mountains. We passed through the mountains and were now to have a two-hour delay in the city of Calgary, in the Province of Alberta. The steam engines and trains needed tending to. There was a pool hall close by and I got to talking with a boy about my own age. We hurried through a game of snooker and soon realized we were going to the same boot camp. Back on the train, the journey was far more fun now.

We had a lot of common interests, except there was one thing that clearly upset him – he missed home already and could not understand my own jubilance at being so free. Those tough years gone by were going to come in mighty handy for me I mused. We left the foothills of the Rocky Mountain range and Calgary, to the wheat growing province of Saskatchewan. I was totally amazed at how flat and how far the eye could see, and now I knew why they called this huge area the Prairies. As I looked out the curved windows of this magnificent domed railway car, my thoughts reflected images of my young life gone by. I listened to the familiar *clickety clack* as each length of track was gobbled up as we sped eastward and the smoke billowed into the clear, crisp, blue sky. I pondered how lucky I was to have lived in British Columbia near the great Pacific Ocean, where the mountains seemed to meet the sky itself and every turn was a new adventure. The train crossed Saskatchewan and was tearing up the track in the province of Manitoba like there was no tomorrow. It was a frightful sight looking out the windows. Blustery winds were whipping the snow into a frenzy and visibility was almost non-existent. I remarked to my new friend that at least we had tracks to follow, and he chuckled. We agreed the clothes I had were not suited for this climate and we both wondered if the Military would supply appropriate clothing.

The time went by and we were then passing through the province of Ontario, far different than the prairie provinces. Not a flat tundra, far more activity and people. It was still damn cold compared to Vancouver, British Columbia. Ottawa, the capital city of Canada is where the Parliament Buildings for the Federal Government tries hard to conduct the affairs of the Nation. I was not politically motivated, even though I was aware of all the major players. The only difference today is the flies have changed but the pile has only gotten bigger. Over seventy hours had been left on the rails behind us and we were in the train station in the City of Montreal, province of Quebec, a bilingual province. I would get a chance to try out my high school French. Military personnel ushered us on to a small bus and we were off to boot camp at a place called St-Jean. This is where I met some other young guys, and we became life-long friends. After another medical test, dental exam, and new hairstyle, we were introduced to Sergeant Wilder, who would be our instructor for the eight-week training program. Our course was the last one of 1956, and hence called fifty-six fifty-one. Rigorous paper testing, physical training, abundant needles, and fainting spells were going on. Some young guys could not cope, either homesick or could just not cut it. They got their wish and were sent home. With my background it was a piece of cake and I treasured almost every moment. No matter what the weather or how you felt, we marched and drilled over and over again. I came to understand the term 'separate the men from the boys.

We had permission to leave the base for Rest and Rehab. I went with some of the older guys who were aged twenty to twenty-five. I soon found out that I needed practice to drink with some of these guys and the smoke from their cigarettes just about did me in. 'Goody two shoes' I was not, but smoking and drinking had never been a priority to me. That day I awoke back at base, promising no more of that shit – at least till I got older. Graduation day arrived. I still, to this day, feel very proud of course 56- 51. There was a marching band. Our uniforms were creased and our boots dazzled the eyes. The white webbing and brass. The way we could handle the M-I Rifles in a drill. When Sergeant Wilder gave the command "Eyes Right" as we marched past our Commanding Officer and other dignitaries, I thought my heart would burst through my chest. It was to be one of the proudest moments of my life. Our group was to be split up and we went our different ways for specialty training.

The aircraft engine course I had decided on was delayed for three months and I was sent on contact training. To my amazement, I was going to Manitoba. Remember the Prairies? Anyway, I am back on the train – this time in uniform and heading west. I got off the train in Winnipeg, the capital city of Manitoba. *God, it was cold!!!* I put my great coat on, which was part of military issue, and thought, "That's better". I was driven to an Air Force base sixty-five miles north of Winnipeg near the town of Gimli. The Gimli Air Base was used to train NATO Pilots from all over the world on T-33 Jet trainers. NATO stands for North Atlantic Treaty Organization. Training means hands on. No more theory, for now at least. I was issued parkas, boots, and snowsuits. My mission was to pay attention and get to know the aircraft they had to fly, no matter what the weather.

* * *

I barely remember this because I simply was not interested in my past, but a letter arrived for me one day at Gimli. It was from a lady in Australia claiming to be my sister. I completely disregarded this as a mix up – not something I wanted to get involved in. In hindsight, it is worth mentioning.

* * *

I returned from Gimli Air Base to Camp Borden in Ontario. Camp Borden was huge. One half was used for training soldiers for the Army and was run independently from the Air Force side, where I had rejoined some buddies from course 56-51. Together, the four of us completed the Aero-Engine course and graduated together. This training had taken almost a year to complete and even though we had our share of time to investigate this wonderful province, it was time to be free for a little while. I had been to Niagara Falls and Buffalo, New York, Wasago Beach and the Canadian National Exhibition. I even went to Detroit City in the State of Michigan, USA. We decided to drive through the northern United States of America and ended up at the Pacific Ocean on the West Coast of British Columbia, which my friends had never seen.

We had thirty-eight days to complete this adventure, so plans were made. I had been in Toronto a couple of weeks prior to graduation and had met with James Lovick (the man I had called Dad). It was strictly a fluke that he was in Toronto on business, but he was absolutely thrilled to see me and asked all kinds of questions. He did not volunteer information about what happened in the past and I did not ask. It appeared he was kind of proud of me and I was a little puzzled. He showed me to office staff, some who remembered me in the early years and reminded me about the elevator caper. The elevator was operated by the human touch and some claimed that I took control and would not let them board and treated it as my private toy for joy. I flashed them a boyish grin and said, "Gosh I don't remember". Turned out he did not want me hitch hiking and I ended up driving back to base in a 1951 Ford convertible that had belonged to an Army General and was in immaculate condition. It was at this moment I re-entered my first parents' lives, eight years after the Fourth and Alma incident. The trip to the West Coast was fabulous. The car suffered one minor break down near the Continental Divide in the State of Montana. It was the starter motor which we promptly repaired ourselves. On arrival to British Columbia, a telegram advised us to report back to base the quickest way possible. The four of us discussed this and with a great lack of knowledge came to the conclusion they could wait a week. We left the car in good hands, said goodbye to British Columbia, and flew to my buddy's place in Saskatchewan. It was a small town called Lumsden in the middle of nowhere. We met his family who advised us of the trouble we could be in as we were AWOL – away without leave. All leave had been cancelled.

We got to our new airbase in Lachine, Quebec as soon as humanly possible but our luck had run out. The crisis was over and nothing but disobeying orders was thrown our way. It was a lesson to be remembered. Nothing on our record but ten days scraping wax off the floor of the digger with a dinner knife. ('Digger' is a military jail). After spending time in the military base digger, it was off to work in the engine bay rebuilding aircraft engines.

I became aware of a flight on the new Jet-propelled passenger aircraft named the Mark 2 Comet and it was leaving Uplands Airport in two days for Vancouver. Somehow, the Sergeant in charge of the engine bay arranged for me to go. Upland Airport was in Ottawa, 120 miles away but as luck would have it, I hitched a ride with no problem. On the way to Upland Airport I could hardly believe what I saw, proven history in the making. A flash of white as the Jet climbed incredibly fast left me awestruck. I was told on arrival it was the Canadian made military AVRO Jet made right here in Canada.

A short time later I was boarding and mingling with VIPs on the Comet Mark 2, four engine air-force Jet liner, another first in my young life as a mere airman. Never in my life had I been so close to dreaming of being so lucky. The big silver bird took off, soon climbing over thirty-thousand feet and upon arrival to Winnipeg, the pilot had to take a second try at landing as the runway was short.

I had signed up to serve for three years and was on my way to a good trade. I learned how to drink beer, party, travel, and fly often, which I thoroughly enjoyed. It was sure that you flew on the Aircraft you worked on. Four Thirteen Squadron "Air Transport Command" made me proud and taught me to pay attention to detail. My roommate friend was spitting blood and had ulcers at eighteen years old. My party was over, and I decided not to re-enlist. I was back to civilian life, a little older, and somewhat wiser. I will never forget my time in the Royal Canadian Air Force. The sad news came when Prime Minister John Diefenbaker ordered the AVRO Arrow fighter Jet destroyed, along with all of the plans. Canadians were sure not happy with dear John.

CHAPTER TWELVE: MR. BERKEFIELD

I drove home to British Columbia from eastern Canada. I never carried on with my Aero Engine trade, as most anywhere paid far more money than being an apprentice. This was a mistake. I was twenty-one, full of vigor, and felt I had done a lot for my age. I was anxious to get my 1951 Ford convertible back on the road. We pushed the car out of the hay barn where it had been stored and in no time at all, it was cleaned up and running. Off to the beach with the top down and radio speakers blaring. In 1961 the economy was booming, and jobs were plentiful. I worked as a production worker in a brand-new Copper Mill. The money was good, but it was not my future. The noise and accident rates were both high and I managed to lose a fingertip to remind me of the ever-present danger of foundry work.

One day, the foreman Doug said, "There is a government guy out by the main entrance that has to see you, but don't be long now." I went out and met the man. He was going on about joining my mother and father in Australia. Nothing he said made sense. I looked at him with disbelief and told him "That's impossible. I have to get back to work". He suggested we meet that evening to which I agreed, as the curiosity was killing me. I gave him my address. The evening came and went, then weeks, and then months. I never heard from the man again. More stress had now been placed on me and I was completely confused and curious. I pushed the thoughts over the horizon of my mind to be drawn back at a later date.

* * *

I obtained a copy of the report he did for his superior over forty years later. He lied to me then and he lied in his report. Time would tell me that my parents had never set foot on Australian soil. I wondered why these Government people were still hounding me after all the anguish they had put me through. G.M. Berkefield, a District Superintendent, filed the report to appease his boss, Mr. C.F. Cornwall, and old documents support this theory. In reality, Mr. Berkefield had met with my ex-foster mother Mona Childs, who had absolutely nothing to do with my life in 1961. I was self-supporting and had no connections to this harsh woman anymore. I did remain a good friend with her son Bill, till his passing fifty years later. Apparently, Mona had gone out of her way to make me out to be some kind of a reckless, uncaring animal.

She obviously lied through her teeth, as all other reports on my young life were contrary to her stories. As an old, divorced widow, I believe she was unhappy that my life had taken a turn for the good. I have had the same wife for over forty years, and I feel sorry for the lonely and deceitful Mona. Fortunately, most people will never know or have to go through the stressful gauntlet of life that I was dealt. Generally, people in my life treated me well, but it was never a substitute for what I lacked – love. Till death, the fear and emotional challenge of my childhood, youth, and adult life haunts my mind. *Why was I cut from loved ones and branded?* Only God can tell me.

CHAPTER THIRTEEN: THE YUKON

The time came and I realized my future was not going to be spent in a Foundry or anything to do with a Production Mill, period. I was reading the paper one day and there was an advertisement calling for guys to go north and make their stake. Before you knew it, a young friend (Ed) and myself were airborne and on the way to the Yukon Territory, north of British Columbia. We should have done a job study before signing on for six months. We landed in a small aircraft in a field of sorts near Dawson City, famous from the Gold Rush days. I believe the hit song 'Squaws along the Yukon' originated there. We were to be driven sixty-five miles or so due North into what was called the Tundra. It was March, so it was more or less light all the time. I did not like it already. It was not at all like the Military where everything and everybody were neat and clean. I thought to myself, "What in the shit have you done this time"? We were so young compared to these men that seemed to speak every language in the world except fluent English. I thought, "This is a place where work sucks, but this time I don't need the bucks!" Ed felt the same. We went to work where we devised our plan to get the hell out of there.

All day long we connected twenty-foot sections of six-inch pipe together. Water would eventually go through the pipes to a dredge which moved ever so slowly, sluicing out the gold from the Tundra; hence, it was called placer or surface gold mining. The only thing I care to remember about that place was the Northern Lights, which were spectacular. Our solution to leaving this terrible land was easy – quit. Well, the boss was not happy to hear that and he told us there was no way out, we were miles from nowhere. I told him I would die trying, as it was like being sentenced to hell to work in such a place. The next day we started walking. I thought about the twelve dollars I had in my pocket. I had lost over two hundred in a poker game the first night in camp, and Ed only had four dollars. We walked and walked – remember, it was light out all the time. Finally, we made a soft spot in the bush and, cool as it was, tried to grab some sleep. Sometime later, we heard the noise of an engine in the distance and it was heading our way. It was a truck from another camp heading into Dawson City. *Man, we felt lucky!* Especially when the driver said he usually made that run the following week. He was a great guy and gave us important information as to what lay ahead of us. Dawson City was the end of the line with him. We thanked him and said good-bye. We checked Dawson City out. It was still very much the way it had been during the Gold Rush days and you could almost feel the excitement of yesteryear.

I had enough to buy some bread, pork, and beans, which we wolfed down cold. We had a look at a couple of old paddle wheelers that used to ply the Yukon River. They had certainly seen better days, but so had we. We found ourselves in an old shack by the river and decided to spend time there for a sleep. The shack would act as a windbreaker. I was sure glad we had heavy coats. Looking back, our youth certainly played a major part in what could have been a tragic adventure. The rest was good, and we decided to get under way by simply following the road signs. Walking with renewed vigor, we headed out of town on the main road. A police car drove by us, slowed quickly, and turned around to see what we were up to. When I told him our story, he treated us very well. The next thing you knew, we were riding in style with the heater going and with the Alaska Highway and the vast expanse of Tundra slipping behind us. I thought of my convertible waiting for me and I felt a feeling of warmth inside. All good rides come to an end. The Mountie dropped us off and wished us well, as he turned off the main highway and disappeared in the distance. He had mentioned we were about two hundred and twenty miles north of Whitehorse, the capital city of the Yukon Territory.

The journey south was a lot different than the flight up there had been, and my partner was starting to grumble and mumble, "A guy could die out here". I was not too impressed myself, but I reassured him that one day we would look back at this and recall the hardship and the challenge of the Alaska Highway. "After all," I thought, "we don't have to take orders from anybody". We were as free as the Eagles that soared overhead, or the Grizzly Bears and Moose that we would encounter from a distance. Sleeping just off the road in the bush became tiresome, but there was nothing better. One morning I was shaving my peach fuzz beard when my nose directed me to the distinct smell of bacon. I followed the scent like a hungry bear. I could not believe my eyes, if we had walked just a tad further around the curve we would have been amongst fellow human beings. The recreational vehicles were impressive. The Americans invited us for breakfast and we ate heartily. Stories were exchanged and we bid them a safe journey to Alaska. They gave us some sandwiches for the road ahead. That's the way it was back then, and we truly thanked them.

We started our march south again, and within an hour we had a ride. This time it was with the Superintendent of some kind of Micro-Tower construction. It was all Greek to me, but as the miles of beautiful scenery went by like a never-ending tapestry, I got the hang of what the towers would do for the future. He fed us and let us stay at the main camp, where we slept on a real mattress. After a hearty breakfast, we were in the station wagon again all the way to Whitehorse. Good-byes and many thanks were given and there we were, once again facing the never-ending ribbon of mostly graveled Alaska Highway. It was still at least a couple hundred miles to the border that divided the Yukon Territory and the Province of British Columbia. Between walking and accepting rides on anything that had wheels (beggars can't be choosers) we made our way to Watson Lake. When we arrived, I rejoiced. Right there was a frontier kind of hotel and I could smell the kitchen. I thought "Ahh, a place to have a good wash, a hamburger, and a beer". I sat down, which was the next best thing to heaven. My buddy was still in the washroom. A big man dressed in white came and offered to take my order. I told him I would wait for my friend, Ed. He started to ask questions, and he was eager to hear my story. Ed came and we ordered beer and hamburgers. The man joined us for a beer and explained that he owned the place, and this would be his treat. Those Northern people were a breed of their own, and I shall never forget that man (even though I can't recall his name forty years later).

A bus had pulled in and was heading south, the passengers had eaten and were boarding. The bus was not full and our new friend who knew the driver had arranged a free ride for the next six hundred miles. I promised to send him a card, and indeed I did, months later. The bus rattled its way over the highway and I felt in seventh heaven as I had the whole back seat to stretch and doze in. Hours later the driver pulled over at the outer limits of Fort St. John, a small northern community. He did not want trouble for giving us a six-hundred-mile free lift. He wished us a safe journey. Feeling quite refreshed, we were on the road again. Rides came quicker now, as there was more traffic on the highway. Drivers back then were not afraid to pick up hitchhikers. As we all know, today it's a different story as the whole world has changed dramatically. A young guy about our age picked us up, which was great as we understood each other's lingo. His name was Randy, and he worked on the oil rigs. He said he made good money and loved the North Country. The pickup truck he drove was tough and in one piece, but hard to tell the color through the mud and grime the roads had treated it to. It was getting close to spring breakup and restrictions would be placed on sections of the road that were paved, so heavy equipment could not travel until the frost left the ground.

I was reminded of when I was in the Air Force in Gimli Manitoba, and it reinforced my opinion that the North Country was beautiful and basically untouched but it was a little too remote for me. I wondered back then, how long it would be until man screwed this wilderness paradise into oblivion, and the last frontier would disappear. Randy pulled into a restaurant in a place called Chetwynd. We had been on the road just over an hour, but it was time to say good-bye again. Although hard to believe, we still had money to spend on burgers and fries. I should mention, the seasons were back, and we had dark nights once again. Our next ride was in a tanker truck and the cargo was oil. The driver was probably in his thirties and he was complaining of being tired, but he had to get south to Prince George. He asked me to make sure he did not nod off and keep the conversation going. It was dark and I didn't have a clue where I was. It turned out it was probably the second scariest ride in my life.

* * *

I forgot to mention, when I was in the Air Force, we decided to go swimming at two o'clock in the morning at a place called Silver Lake in the province of Quebec. I was a passenger, along with three other Airmen, and we were feeling no pain. The driver somehow lost control of the 1949 hopped-up Mercury Coupe and we smashed into a concrete wall at well over seventy miles per hour. Obviously, we all should have died. Three of us were battered and bruised, but okay. The driver was not so lucky, as he spent almost a year in hospital. I often think if I had a seatbelt on that night, I would have died at the scene. Fortunately, two of us were thrown clear. Mona (one of my foster mothers) used to screech *"Only the good die young"!* Well, she is eighty years old now. So much for that theory.

* * *

As the tanker truck barreled through the dark, loosely guided by an overtired driver, I thought "Shit! Don't think of that now". Of course, I didn't know then, but years later I would barrel up and down that same highway and would often think of that awesome ride through what they called the Peace River Country. The huge truck pulled into a truck stop on the outskirts of the city of Prince George. It was ten days ago that our aircraft had landed at the Prince George Airport and we were full of piss and vinegar with dreams of our future riches, as we headed further north to the Yukon. Now we are back in Prince George and a meager five hundred miles from home. The trucker thanked me for riding with him and staying awake while Ed slept. We went inside the truck stop for a wash, toast, and coffee. I went for a wash first and Ed said he would order. Well, let me tell you what happened next! I had washed up, felt refreshed, and as I entered the main diner, I scanned the room but could not see Ed. A quick look out the window revealed a milk tanker truck with *him* in it, pulling onto the highway heading south for the Pacific Coast and home. I felt devastated and pissed off, after all we had done together. I had to contain the choice words that I wanted to shout out to anyone who would listen. Instead, I ordered toast and coffee and decided I should have been on my own the entire journey from that barren wasteland that wasn't fit for man nor beast. Ed had no pizzaz, people, or survival skills. I swore him off as a friend for good.

I left the restaurant and my thumb got to work begging for a ride. Within minutes, a sleek and shiny Volkswagen Beetle pulled over and I heard a voice yell, "C'mon kid, ya think I got all day". I had never ridden in a Beetle before. Sitting so low, it seemed like I could touch the pavement. Overall, I was truly impressed with this tiny car, and apparently so was the driver. I would guess him to be in his early thirties and he was dressed to the nines. He was great to bullshit with, but my lifelong training and skills were evaluating him as we sped down the highway to a town called Quesnel, where he said he had to make a stop. I could carry on hitchhiking or stop with him and then carry on all the way to the coast, which was home. The decision was easy. We pulled off the highway and went a fair way down a gravel road, then turned on to a long, well-kept private driveway. All of a sudden, we broke out into a cleared off area and right smack in front of us was a home that belonged in a magazine. Certainly, I thought, it belonged to somebody very rich. I was rubber necking in every direction, completely in awe, when a voice said, "Who's the kid?". My eyes focused in the direction of the sound, and I was looking at a huge man as his eyes gave me the once over. I firmly met his gaze and showed no fear. The driver (who had said his name was Larry) spoke up and everything seemed cool. The big guy invited me in the house and directed a young woman to feed me. He and Larry disappeared to another part of the mansion. About an hour went by and the men reappeared.

The woman was instructed by the big guy to make them a sandwich, which she did willingly. It was obvious they were not married. But, *What the hell did I care?* They treated me good. Larry had filled the big fella in a bit as to my story, and he seemed quite relaxed as we made small talk. Soon we were back in the Beetle heading for the highway and Larry said, "Kid, do you want a job?" I replied, "What doing?" Larry explained that I would be a delivery man, and details would be discussed another time back at the mansion if I accepted. In the meantime, I was to take my time, get my shit together, and phone him at the phone number he had provided when I was ready. He said the big man liked the fact that I had no ties to anything or anybody and he liked my easy manner. I tried hard, without pressing or sounding like a bug, to find out more and also the name of the big fella. That was a waste of time. Although, he did tell me he had spent some time in jail. Larry also said, "You don't wear alligator shoes and dress like *this* working for a living". I knew all along that something shady was in the offering and I also knew it would be hard to say no.

We were driving through a place called Cache Creek. There was a junction where the highway was joined by another highway heading to a place called Kamloops. The tanker truck that Ed had slipped away in must have turned for Kamloops, leaving Ed to seek another ride. Larry slowed down and pulled onto the shoulder of the road, as I had told him what the creep had done. Ed came running for his ride, which was not to be. I made sure he recognized me as I gave him the 'one finger salute' and Larry shot back onto the highway, both of us laughing. I never saw the guy again. Within a couple of hours, I would be home and crash into a familiar bed in the little cabin in the woods that I alone, could use. Larry drove me almost to where I was going, but I did not want him to know this secret cabin, as I still did not know the business he was in. We shook hands and I promised I would be in touch. It was a promise I did not keep, and to this day I wonder how one phone call could have changed my life. I mused to myself "Shit, I ain't all bad". I got up very refreshed, some fourteen hours later.

CHAPTER FOURTEEN: SHERYL

I got a job as a chainman with a land surveyor and learned all about geodetic benchmarks – how to tie properties together or subdivide them and to set grade boards on construction sites for new pipelines and roads. Working for the same corporation, I was approached about entering the field of water works, pumps and controls, high pressure testing, leak detection and chlorinating of old and new water mains and towers. Eagerly, I accepted this brand-new challenge to learn this young technology. Sheryl, my future wife, worked as a cashier in the Overwaitea food store in Cloverdale.

Our first short meetings consisted of me pestering her at the cash register, but that soon turned into a date away from the casual encounters at the store. Sheryl and her younger sister Margaret had been raised by their grandparents – I am not sure why, to this day. As time went by and I spent more time with Sheryl, the light shone brighter in my eyes. A strange feeling entered my heart and our lives started to intertwine as we shared our life stories that both held so many blanks throughout our childhoods. We discovered that we loved to dance together, especially to country western and rock n' roll. We often drove south across the border to a small town called Blaine in the American state of Washington, to listen and dance to Loretta Lynn (a future Queen of Country music) at Bill's Tavern.

Sheryl accompanied Loretta now and then, as she also had magic in her voice that I would still hear many years later. It appeared that God had returned my childhood call after all, providing us with love, family, and the tools to build a life together. I should add that Sheryl is a wonderful cook, and believe me when I say, "It wasn't God that made Honky Tonk Angels!" I married Sheryl in 1963, much to the amazement of all our friends. They thought I was far too wild and that it would never last. The Royal Canadian Legion in Cloverdale supplied the hall for free and one of the local bands, our friends, supplied the music. Sheryl's sisters and friends put on a meal fit for a king. There were few gifts, for our friends decided if we lasted six months, we would receive the gift of a lifetime. Except for one dear friend, Sheryl and I are still waiting for those gifts thirty-eight years later. I had no family to offer my young wife, so she shared her family with me. Luckily, I was accepted forever by all of them, and I was glad her maiden name was Smith.

We purchased our first home a month after we were married, and I was some proud of our new acquisition. It was an overgrown one-acre parcel with the oldest rundown house you could hope to see. In our eyes (well, in mine anyway) I saw the makings of a castle. I thought my new brother-in-law, Teddy Bear as we called him, would help and guide me through my dream. He was older, wiser, and one hell of a good carpenter by trade. Sheryl's Mum and sisters were put to the task of cleaning and painting the palace before this king and his young wife would move in. The beautiful wood stove supplied our heat, hot water, and the only cooking facility where my wife would bake the best bread this side of heaven. I stopped in one day after work to see how the crew were getting on with the painting and cleaning. They had the wood stove pouring out the warmth they required. It was all very cozy, and the turn-of-the-century furniture and old pictures that came with the house did not look quite so morbid. I made a mental note that all that junk would go as soon as we could afford to do so. All at once there was a roaring sound, and the girls all looked at me. "Chimney fire, get outside!", I yelled. Once outside, I jumped and cleared the fence to the neighbours. Our neighbour, Mrs. Collins had seen through her window and had already called the fire department. I quickly thanked her and returned home. We could hear the sirens coming. The first thing the firemen did was take control and assure all of us that the old house would survive.

They simply let the fire burn itself out in the chimney, then checked things out. One fireman returned the next day and gave the okay to light the stove. He said we had saved the price of a chimney sweep. I had heard the sound of a chimney fire at one of the cottages at the orphanage on Vancouver Island many years before. The girls were totally amazed at how I cleared the fence to reach the neighbor to sound the alarm. *Quite frankly, so was I.* That old house was our home for seven years. Over the years it acquired more occupants, namely two daughters, two dogs, and a cat. We also added a couple of pigs to raise our own pork, thanks to my friend Ron. The idea was great until it was time to take piggy to market. Ron's boys thought the pork was great. All our girls did was cry, looking at their pets wrapped in brown paper. Ron thought it was hilarious.

The house had received some updates but it was still old and now, too small. We sold and bought more acreage about twenty miles east in the Fraser Valley. It was a pretty place with a creek running through the property that was loaded with Rainbow Trout. Our oldest girl, Vicki, spent many hours fishing West Creek in her little boat we got for her. Teddy built us a new ranch style house, and it seemed like heaven. We had a pasture, and we bought the girls horses. Every kid seemed to have a horse back then. The creek entered into a pond that was damned up by beavers, and if the winter weather was right, we could ice skate and play scrub hockey to our hearts' content. Along with the horses there were four dogs of different breeds, ducks that we called the happy gang, and a couple of cats that did a nice job outside. They all got along with no bother. If only the girls could have done the same. They were as different as night and day. Vicki would help dad and Brenda helped Mum. Sometimes, all three would turn on me and I would wish that I had stayed single when my pockets did jingle. Being much older now, I treasure those memories and wish we could play it over just one more time. The years sped by and the girls got married, each one having two sons.

CHAPTER FIFTEEN: SHOCKING NEWS

Two grown up daughters and four grandsons later, we fast forward to 1992. My wife Sheryl and I had just gotten home from a trip to the Grand Old Opera in the U.S. state of Tennessee. It was the biggest time of year for country music fans and a dream come true for Sheryl, as we also toured Elvis Presley's Graceland in Memphis.

We had bought a new house before the trip and faced a lot of work with the packing and moving as our possession date was here. Plus, we had to sell the home we were in. It was time to roll up the shirtsleeves. I had formed a plan in order of priority to get through this. Well, the phone rang, and it would literally change my life forever. The caller had a strange accent and claimed he was Peter, my sister Janet's son from Australia. *Talk about a drum roll going through my head!* I had to take a moment and get my bearings. Peter said he was in Vancouver at Jericho hostel. He had looked in a phone book, looked up the Isherwood name, and called to see if he might be related. I decided to meet him, and when we met, I was overwhelmed at the resemblance we shared.

The big test was when I phoned and talked to Peter's mother, Janet. I asked her a key question that would put my mind at ease that this was not a joke. I asked, "What was the name of the horse at Middlemore Homes?" "Babs." she said. That was the correct answer, which she could have only known if she had been at Middlemore. The clouds of my childhood would not dissipate and I became very angry with people I would never know. Between Peter and Janet, I learned about my other brother and sisters in Australia. It sounds like they had a shitty life at The Fairbridge called Pinjarra in West Australia. The light of a new dawn came, and my brain recalled my younger brother Joe and some contact we had in the past. It is so sad that one cannot get a second lease on life, but the beat must go on. Peter stayed for a week and we had a good time visiting. Peter and brother Joe had government jobs, and sister Janet was a nurse. Another sister, Margaret, was a homemaker. My phone bill increased dramatically as other unknown family members joined the list. Sheryl and I started to think about a trip to Australia, and I started to check things out.

Some people at work knew a bit about my dilemma and I was often prone to some teasing. *Can you imagine this?* My work supervisor, Ralph, who was due to retire, remarked "Isherwood, are you sure you're a Canadian Citizen? It could affect your pension, you know!" I chortled, "Of course, I am, the Government was my legal guardian and I served in the Royal Canadian Air Force, just like you." Ralph retired, and quite some time later I thought about checking into the details of receiving my pension. This turned into a nightmare of huge proportions. First of all, a lot of the information required on the forms they sent me I could not answer. After all, the Government should have had records of me and they should have supplied and filled in the blanks. After a great length of time, I received a reply from Immigration Canada. They explained to me that I did not exist on any Government records, and they wondered what I was doing in this country. I received this news on August 12, 1992. At first, I tried putting the whole thing out of sight and out of mind. This was easier said than done. Whether I liked it or not, it was the dawning of an age. I could not ignore this very confusing situation. So, I tried to move heaven and earth (with no help) to put my mind at rest.

The process was extremely stressful for me and the more I found out, the quicker doors were slammed in my face. I wrote a letter to Middlemore Homes in England and received a reply months later. They included a copy of a Migration Identification Card. This proved that indeed, I was a landed Immigrant in Halifax, Nova Scotia May 25, 1947. I also tried to get help from two members of parliament, to no avail. One of them even suggested to me that there were lots of 'War Babies' and basically "so sad, big deal". If he had the decency of granting me a phone call, I would have told him that he didn't know what the hell he was talking about. His name is not worth mentioning, but I have his reply in writing. I would never vote for this man who makes a big noise and is all show and no substance. This was simply another case of people not caring and not being interested in finding out what was really going on.

CHAPTER SIXTEEN: CANADIAN CITIZEN

My letter to Ottawa - January 14, 1998:

* * *

I have a story to tell you about Social Services (formerly Children's Aid Society).

I have been involved in the government bureaucracy since early 1940's. I was born in Birmingham, England December 23, 1938. I did the entire Second World War as a child in England. In 1947, the Canadian Federal Authority gave the okay to bring me to Canada. I ended up in a place called Fairbridge Farm Schools at Duncan, Vancouver Island, a place for underprivileged British children. I arrived at Duncan, I believe, in March of 1947. We did the religion, farm work and school, ate off tin dishes mainly in a mess hall.

About 1950, I was placed in the home of James and Marjorie Lovick for adoption. Didn't work out. However, I am still in touch with Marjorie who is now a Harris and still resides in the Kerrisdale area of Vancouver, British Columbia. After the Lovick's I was off to a number of foster homes, farms etc., where I carried on with more work. Fortunately, I liked school and did fairly well, although I attended many.

At fifteen years of age, I was on my own basically, in a boarding home in Maple Ridge, B.C., still going to school and working weekends and holidays.

At seventeen years old I decided to join the RCAF, with testing and government approval (my legal guardian), it was a done deal.

In December 1963, I married my wife Sheryl. We raised two daughters who each have two sons. It turns out though, fifty years later, I was talked into checking to see if I was a Canadian citizen. The answer I received was negative.

I decided to check things out through the Freedom of Information Act. My first contact was with the B.C. Archives. Their final response was I did not exist on any government records from 1947 to 1955. Tough luck. I then contacted Middlemore Homes in Birmingham, England to find out what on earth happened to me, (e.g., Why was I brought here? Especially when I was in England for the entire war, nothing makes sense).

Middlemore replied, finally. I was sent to Canada and my brother and three sisters were sent to Australia. In one document the Canadian Federal Authorities say it was not desirous to split the children. It turns out that I wasn't orphaned after all. Documents say my father protested violently as to my whereabouts. He died in 1947, months after I was shipped to Canada and my mother died in 1975. Why wasn't I told about her?

I got a hold of the local MLA, Fraser Valley East, to see if he could help me with this citizenship problem. This took the better part of a year to tell me something I already knew, make an application and pay $200.00. Personally, to me, it adds salt to the wound. I feel that I should not have to pay 2 cents.

This government deprived me of my childhood, they have deprived my children and their children of knowing their grandmother, aunts, uncles and cousins. I've voted in every election since I decided to vote many, many moons ago. I am working for the Federal government – Matsqui Institution in Abbotsford, B.C., for many years now.

I spent time in the RCAF. I've always been proud to be a Canadian - now I'm not so sure after finding out so many negative things that went on behind the scenes within the Children's Aid Society. I'm not asking for anything I don't deserve. I want the government to grant my Canadian citizenship so the Canadian family I have can have a Canadian Dad and Grandpa.

Thank you for your attention in this matter.

Tom Isherwood

* * *

This letter was mailed directly to the Immigration Minister of Canada. The Honorable Lucienne Robillard, elected by the people to serve the people. Another joke used by stand-up comics. Here I am literally begging for help and I have probably been in this country longer than most of that sorry lot. I wonder how much time this Member of Parliament, who would not give me the time of the day, served in the Military for his country? Funny but this "War Baby" as he referred to me, has been there and done that. Plus, I did the Second World War before he was barely born. I excuse you for your lack of knowledge, among other things I find distasteful. On June 15, 1998 (five months after sending my plea for help) the Honorable Lucienne Robillard asked somebody to reply to this mere 'mortal'. The letter stated that I should be pleased to learn Immigration Canada has been able to locate pertinent information pertaining to my arrival in Canada. Funny *they have never offered to share this information with me.* I suggested the only information they had was what I supplied them with – namely, a copy of my Immigration Identification Card stamped May 25, 1947 (when I was 8 years old and had no say in my own life). *Gee!*

Finally, through sheer frustration and anger I gave in. The practically empty application for Citizenship was reluctantly sent to Ottawa to Citizen Case Review Attn: Roesmarie Redden. On my insistence, I had a very private crossing from whatever I was, to becoming a Citizen of Canada. On July 21, 1998, my wife Sheryl, a very nice Judge, and myself were in this huge room that could obviously seat several hundred people. It was eerie to say the least. Things were going well until we got to the part about swearing allegiance to the Queen and my mouth all of a sudden felt like it was stuffed with cotton batten. My whole body felt cold and unresponsive. The Judge sensed my anxiety, and I explained my reasoning as I felt the older members of the Royal family were also guilty of war crimes against their own babies. They had to know what was going on in those awful places that were called the 'Homes'. I muffled unintelligibly the rest of the way through, until finally I received the certificate signed by Lucienne Robillard herself. The last words on the certificate stated, "Welcome to the Canadian Family". *MY GOD!* I could have broken out in a nervous laugh as I thought "There's a good chance I have belonged to this Family longer than she has!" I thanked the Judge and went outside and breathed in fresh Canadian air for the first time as a Canadian Citizen. *Can you just imagine the thrill I got?* I did not have to wave that tiny flag with the Maple Leaf on it. The same kind of flag that has flown from my small boat for many years. I remember way back when the Maple Leaf was chosen to represent Canada as a Nation. I can only guess you got tired of the Union Jack along with the name Dominion of Canada. You were seeking what I still seek – identity... and my family back. Or, at the very least, communication, truth, and the records I needed so badly.

* * *

I stayed in touch with my sister Janet in Australia and learned a lot about their trials and tribulations. They were shipped off to a strange land without a choice too. Beryl, Margaret, Janet, Thomas, and Joseph were born in that order. Thomas (me) was shipped to Canada on his own in May 1947. The other four were shipped like cattle (around 1950) to the other side of the world. Funny how the British said, "It was not desirous to split the children, and if it should happen, great pain would be taken to reunite them". What they did was hide their war crimes against their own little babies from the world. That is until recently. The world is coming out of a deep slumber and is astonished and sick at what Britain has done.

My own flesh and blood fought for your stinky little country, some giving up their lives. Others, to return home only to find the little ones they loved and cared for nowhere to be found. *Why the hell did they fight the war? So, the rich and royal could go on living their dream?* History tells me the crusades were over long ago. America tells me there is a better way, and that's the way I have been taught. Not to freeload, but to make your own way.

As I write, my three uncles and their families don't even know my family or me. My uncles are alive and well and vaguely remember their nephew, Thomas, and being off to war. They cannot tell me much about the home front. You see, I did more days of war in England than they did. My thrill now is when I get the odd letter, or I phone now and then and wonder if we shall live long enough to meet and have a reunion of closure. Nineteen ninety-six came along and something told me to have another go at it, so I contacted the British Columbia Archives in the Capital City of Victoria. This place was not far away from the Fairbridge Farm School where now I could pretend, I played the part of Oliver Twist when I was there; after all, it could seem but a dream to some. I wish that were so. I received mail dated December 3, 1996, from MacCulham, Manager of Information and Privacy Section, BC Archives and Records Service. By law, they had thirty days to respond to my request for records under the *Freedom of Information and Protection of Privacy Act*. I had sent my request by fax and felt impressed by the quick response.

This was to be short lived, and the beginning of a nightmare. The Deputy Provincial Archivist writes, "We have located your file but public access to them is restricted to the year 2035. You will note, that with the exception of your Immigration Identification Card, these records date from 1955 to 1961, after the time you left Fairbridge Farm School". This information was absolutely useless, as I was 17 years old in 1955. My memory in 1955 was excellent, as it is today. The only good thing that came out of this set of records search; it reinforced the memory as to the horrible way my teen years were handled. I was more determined than ever to seek the truth from day one, and this I would do with a vengeance. One could never dream the sadness that lay ahead, and the rejection I would be subjected to. None of which I created but suppose I shall be punished with till the day I die. *Who are the real Bastards? Would you please step forward?* They say things can get worse before they get better. I strongly disagree when it comes to government and its bureaucracy.

I ask however, if the only files on record are from 1955 to 1961, what happened to the records of my arrival in 1947, up until 1955, and why are the documents sealed? Why was the year 2035 chosen? Perhaps it is because all of us Fairbridge kids will be gone from this Earth by then. What is it they are trying to hide?

CHAPTER SEVENTEEN: RECONNECTING

Sometime in April of 1999, my sister Janet sent a news release copy that she had acquired from British Information Services Australia. It stated, March 31, 1999 *"UK Government announces Child Migrant Fund"* to assist Child Migrants to reunite with family. My first thought was, "Sounds very well, but for many migrants, too little too late". The fires of war were put out and rebuilding had taken place. In the Child Migrant's heart, the fires will smolder till eternity. You offer a crumb and believe that two weeks out of a lifetime with their own flesh and blood will repair the tattered hearts and souls of the children you convicted and banished from their homeland? And you expect me to swear allegiance to what I now believe is a foreign country? "Forget it, as you forgot me". As usual in Canada, you have to rely on another country to guide the way. Curiously, I sent a letter to the Canadian address supplied by my Australian sister, Janet.

On May 17, 1999, I received a reply from International Social Services (ISS) Canada in Ottawa, Ontario. Executive Director, Agnes Casselman, said she would send an information package to me as soon as it was available. Even this was confusing, as I received an information package from ISS Australia prior to one from Agnes. I decided to call Agnes on the telephone and ask some hardline questions. It was a good move, as it added a voice to the mail I had received. The kind of voice that I felt had genuine feeling and trust, and as time went by it proved to be so. I was starting to believe that this reunion with my family might become a reality; however, there were pitfalls ahead. Literally having to prove to them from across the seas that yes, indeed we are family. Letters and documents. and written proof that indeed my family wanted to meet up with me, their brother, after all these years of being apart. *Why did they not just add insult to injury and suggest DNA testing?* If you are not one of us, you cannot imagine the anguish and emotional pain they stirred up that had been lying dormant for so many years. Finally, the pieces of the puzzle resembled a picture and I thought "My God, it's going to happen!" Passports were obtained and travel plans were made. I had promised Steve Berry, the newspaper man, ages ago that I would keep him posted on any progress, so I let him know what was happening.

Much to my surprise, Steve did another article headlining, *Little Tommy Isherwood is Going Home*. I was totally unaware of this until I arrived at work and staff members said, "You are in the newspaper again". Well, all I heard for several days was, *"Little Tommy's going home"*. It was all in good fun, and it made me appreciate the caring and support my fellow workers bestowed upon me. I was truly grateful for them, and Agnes from ISS, for their understanding. The months went by and the calendar was flipped to another year and a new millennium. May of 2000 arrived, and we thought a lot about our upcoming journey around the world. I thought to myself, "Why is everything such a battle to begin with? Why don't the people or country responsible for the mess, clean it up?" I hoped my dog Nikita would be alright, as we would be away for five weeks and the mutt was terribly spoiled.

* * *

The morning of May 21, 2000, the weather was cloudy with rain. My wife Sheryl and I were at our home in Abbotsford, about thirty miles east of Vancouver B.C., preparing for our trip. Sheryl did a final check on our baggage and I took Nikita, my Rottweiler dog, for a walk. We would be gone for five weeks and the mutt would surely miss us. My daughter, Brenda, would look after her. Our niece, Mary, would stay at our place till our return. The day flew by and it was time to head for the airport. Our good friends Ron and Josephine (Jose) Remple drove us to the Vancouver International Airport. Brenda, Neil, and our two grandsons, Jimmy and Christopher, followed us. The boys were really excited about the airport terminal, as well as seeing all the aircraft take off and land. After a short time, we said our good-byes. This was the furthest we had ever ventured from our two young grandsons. We boarded a British Airways 747-400 Jumbo Jet – it was huge inside! We felt kind of cramped, even as we taxied out to the runway – not much leg room, even for short legs like mine. The roaring down the runway soon made me forget about my legs. I had a window seat and marveled at the ease in which this machine left the ground behind. We gained altitude as we knifed our way through the clouds. Our destination was London, England. ETA nine hours. The plane reached altitude and passengers settled in for a very pleasant flight. I must say, the flight attendants were highly trained and catered to passengers' every whim. I followed the aircraft's progress on a small monitor attached to the back of the seat in front of me. Movies were also available. It got a little bumpy over Greenland, but most people appeared to sleep right through the turbulence. Unfortunately, neither of us could sleep as the excitement about our long trip ahead seemed to give us renewed vigor.

Soon, we were flying over northern Scotland, and in no time at all the captain reported our final approach. I went to slip my leather dress shoes on and panic set in. My feet had slightly swollen. I managed to squeeze my right shoe on, but the left shoe was a problem. I asked the attendant if there was a shoehorn available, and he came back with a huge soup spoon saying that was the best he could do. I thanked him, and finally wrestled my right foot into my loafer, after taking some skin off my ankle. The gracious attendant assured me it was quite common for feet to swell, as I gave him back his soup spoon. My thoughts were to change footwear, to my Reeboks with air. A smile came over my face thinking of my comfy running shoes. The smile turned to a look of horror as I realized that we had requested all our baggage go direct to Perth, West Australia. I set my watch ahead eight hours just before we touched down and decided to grin and bear it. We were now in Heathrow Airport, London England. We were astonished at the size of this operation. We followed the crowd and signs and cleared customs in a reasonable time. After being away from the country of my birth for fifty-five years, I thought some official would surely appear. It was not to be, and I felt slightly let down. We got turned around in the baggage section, but with some kind directions we ended up on the right floor of this huge terminal.

We scanned the crowd of people, looking for my sister Pat and her husband Rod, neither of whom I had ever met in my entire life. We learned of them through Janet and recognized them from photographs we had exchanged. Our initial meeting was no big show of emotion, as I was over that many years ago. It was more like; *can you tell me what the hell happened to us?* It was a strange moment, but truly exciting. It was hard to refrain from talking over each other, as we all stumbled for the right words. It was hard for me to imagine that I used to have the same accent as them, and now had difficulty understanding my own sister. It was funny, to say the least. We all had a good laugh over 'excusing' each other. All of a sudden, we forgot about being tired. We loaded our luggage into Rod's car and I headed for the passenger door (which over there is the driver's side). We had a chuckle at that, and then food was mentioned. Fish and chips at an Old English Pub was suggested. *Wow! Good idea.* We were off, into a maze of traffic like I had never witnessed before. On top of that, I felt like I wanted to grab the wheel and steer the bloody car to the right side of the road.

We pulled into a gravel parking lot beside the first British Pub we saw. As we entered the pub, it felt like we had been propelled back in time. It was so quaint, and God only knows how old it was. You could almost believe that Prince Valiant would walk through the door. The fish and chips were excellent, along with a pint of English beer. The four of us chatted about anything and everything that entered our minds – no format or rehearsal to go by. There was a natural bond between us that was comfortable, yet surreal. We were about to leave the pub as a young man appeared at the doorway announcing a license plate number. The plate number belonged to my brother in- law's new car. The young man advised Rod that he was parked illegally, and he had placed a wheel lock on the vehicle so it could not move. Rod's car was the only one parked on what turned out to be parking for a bingo hall that was open only in the evenings. Rod was arguing with this guy about the amount of money required before the wheel lock could be moved. I did not understand the English money, so Pat told me roughly what it was in Canadian funds. I almost fainted. It was about a hundred and fifty dollars. This was a scam, and the kid started back tracking on the amount required. Rod paid up and would not hear of me chipping in. Turned out he paid by credit card, cancelled it, took it to court, and won.

That ordeal behind us, we headed into the city. Rod knew his way around quite well but the traffic patterns were still frightening. The English drivers with their hand signals and signs would not fly in North America, but it appeared most drivers seemed quite courteous to each other. As a passenger, it was a unique experience, to say the least. Before we knew it, the four of us were standing in front of the main gates to Buckingham Palace. A flag was flying high up towards the roof. Someone remarked that it meant the Queen was in the castle. That meant little to me, but I did marvel at the architecture. The palace guards caught my attention and I thought that I would not want their job for love nor money. It was painful to think of a Royal Family existing in the modern world. *What was the purpose?* I wondered. *Do they know or care about what happened to small fry like me at the time?* Answer: of course not. I have no feeling for that family whatsoever, and never will. We bid the palace goodbye, after the girls took many snap shots. We did a walking tour of Hyde Park. It too, was beautiful. My damn feet were still aching a little from the swelling and Sheryl reported she was getting tired, so we headed for the car.

We drove by Harrod's Department Store, Piccadilly, and Big Ben. One last stop was at Waterloo Station, where we had to walk to see the activity. It looked to be as busy as Heathrow Airport. My eyes were spinning like two buttons on an outhouse door to try to keep up with all the people going in more than four different directions. It was a sight to behold, and one I shall not soon forget. We arrived at a quaint Bed and Breakfast. Rod had arranged for us to stay here overnight. It was about four kilometers from the airport, and it seemed ideal for our purpose. Rod and Pat faced a two-and-a-half-hour drive north, past the city of Birmingham so it was impossible to stay with them at this time. Sheryl went in to pay for our arrangement and soon returned to say her goodbyes to Rod and Pat. She mentioned that she had paid sixty-five pounds for the room and my hair stood on end. I was holding their brochure and it read forty-five pounds for the rest of the year, 2000. This was May. I went and inquired, but to no avail. The lady at the desk said the rates had just gone up and the brochure meant nothing. I asked her nicely (albeit sarcastically) if somebody had told her we were coming. That comment went way over her head. It was 8:30 pm and we were extremely tired. Sheryl actually felt quite sick, likely from the car ride. The only window in the room looked directly into a back alley where we had a good view of garbage cans. I closed the motley curtain, showered, and set the alarm for 7am.

The next thing we knew, the alarm clock was doing its thing – morning had arrived quickly. I had another shower, got some postcards ready for the mail, checked our baggage (the little we had), and went upstairs for the advertised English Breakfast. The only thing that was English was the nice little waitress, and the country we were having toast in. Rod phoned to make sure we hadn't slept in. We had a quick laugh and said goodbye again. We had the desk call a taxi and they advised us not to pay more than nine pounds for the drive to the airport. A colored man with an English accent drove us to the airport. I had to chuckle inside, as he thought I was a foreigner. I guess I was a 'tourist' in my country of birth. He was a pleasant bloke. When I asked him what we owed, he said ten pounds. I informed him what the clerk at the B&B had told us. It was hard to say if he blushed or not. Heathrow is a big airport – the shops go on forever. Sheryl bought her friend Jose a true English nightgown. I bought a shoehorn, as I thought of my experience the day before. It cost about the same as a pair of shoes would in Canada!

A charming British Airways attendant changed our seats for the flight to Singapore, so we were not directly over the wing of the aircraft. We boarded the magnificent 747 jet and were pleased there was no one sitting between us. There were quite a few empty seats, so it was easy to move around and stretch. The first part of the trip was a little cloudy so there was no view. After lunch the cloud cover lifted and I could see mother earth way down below. It was Germany. Dinner was poached salmon, salad, and (Sheryl says) 'Banoffee pie' – *whatever that is?* Later on, we flew over the tip of Russia and I could see the Baltic Sea. There was a nice couple from Australian sitting behind us that we swapped stories with. That helped peel time from this twelve-and-a-half-hour flight. We had to buckle up over Pakistan, as it was slightly bumpy for a little while. It was dark, but I could see some lights way down below. I wondered what the people were like as we silently made our way through their skies. The long stillness of night passed slowly. The attendant handed out ice cream bars (*Oh great! That was all I needed...*), but I guzzled it back. About an hour away from our landing it started to get light. The view was spectacular! The pilot banked the aircraft to port slightly and we were flying parallel to a lightning storm. As we disappeared into a rotten-looking cloud bank, the seat belt sign went on and the flight became a little bumpy. We came out of the cloud cover to see something absolutely remarkable. Looking down from 36,000 feet, dark was meeting light in the distance. Then the sun popped up, making the clouds look like a huge down quilt with flecks of gold woven through it. I can play this picture in my mind forever, and for that I will be eternally grateful.

We landed in Singapore, Gateway to Asia, and I'm telling you, there is no time to be tired. The temperature was 28 degrees Celsius and we only had half an hour to check the terminal out. Hardly enough time to see such a beautiful site, but we had to catch our final flight to Perth, Australia. The excitement was mounting. We had a very smooth flight to Perth, and were pleased to have met Chad, a real Ozzie. He acted as tour guide as we made our way over northern Australia. The scenery below was amazing, and Chad reminded us we were in the South Pacific with much to see. Before we landed, the attendants came down the aisles with aerosol cans and sprayed every passenger. Some were not too pleased, as there was no prior mention of this, or explanation of what they were spraying. (Strangely, we were not sprayed on our return flight three weeks later.) Sheryl and I made our way through the airport terminal. It was nice, but so small compared to Singapore and Heathrow. Out of a crowd of people we heard distinctly, "There they are!!", and the tears started to flow as we approached them. So many sisters and their grown-up kids! It was a little overwhelming. *Can you imagine?* Everyone was touching and pinching to see if it was real. The same blood ran through their veins as mine. All of this hurt was pouring out after so many years of being torn apart by our birth country, England. To see the physical similarities and gestures and the real love pouring out was very overwhelming – the kind of stuff that energizes your very soul. My own tears were hard come by, but the pain behind my eyes was excruciating and I thought my head would pop. I soon realized that my brother Joe was not there but was told he would join us soon. We had agreed to wave off the media at this time, and that suited me just fine. Derek, a social worker from the Child Migrant Trust, was there to greet us. The Trust was set up to help migrant children reconnect with family, if possible. However, they were of no assistance to the Isherwood family at all in this great reunion. The Isherwood Family did all of this work alone.

* * *

At that time, the Child Migrant Trust did not exist in Canada, as described in the book *'Empty Cradles'* written by Margaret Humphreys, the founder of the Child Migrant Trust. What Humphreys said in her book about Canada I find, is totally untrue and should stand to be corrected. No one has the right to change history on paper, or otherwise.

* * *

Maybe Derek thought we needed special emotional support? I told him via a phone call from Canada that I was well and competent and was looking forward to meeting my family without my knees buckling. I must say however, that Derek was very thoughtful and offered that we stay a night or two in a quaint house nearby, held by the Trust. Sheryl's friend, Jose, back in Canada, would have fallen in love with this dwelling. Construction was early Australian I think, with a distinct English twist. Derek's helper, Sonia, had prepared a late lunch for us with a variety of sandwiches, pickles, chips, etc. including beer and drinks. It was truly decent of them. The other great thing was finding my blue jeans and Reebok running shoes. I now had family and comfort, and then my brother Joe entered the room. There was a hush. It was like looking at a reflection in a pond. More hugging and tears. I was getting tired and I felt some emotions that I had not felt in many years. The clock rolled around, and we had to say good-bye until the next day. Sheryl and I were tired, for sure. Sheryl was up early and had coffee going while admiring all the antique furniture in the house. The fridge was stocked for a fine breakfast and my wife had no problem figuring out the kitchen.

I went for a walk, as it was getting light. I could see the difference between our countries already. *Palm trees and wild parrots!* I raced back to tell Sheryl what I had discovered and was just in time for a lovely breakfast. I would have taken her out for breakfast, but we didn't have a clue as to where we were. I cleaned up the kitchen and Sheryl admired the dry, wild Australian flowers that sister Margaret had given to her, and the fresh cut flowers placed in the house. Derek and Sonia showed up, and we all had coffee and after a nice chat, Derek gave me a book titled, *Empty Cradles,* first published in 1994, and written by social worker Margaret Humphreys. I thanked Derek but had no time to read the book during such a short visit.

* * *

When back at home and reading the sad story of Fairbridge Australia child migrants, the story brought back memories of my own life while existing at Fairbridge Farms near Duncan, British Columbia in Canada. Tears were trying desperately to escape but were held back by my emotional dam created years ago. Reading on I was sent into shock as I read about the whistle stop visit Humphrey made little time for during her visit to Fairbridge Canada! Margret Humphreys own words I quote from her book Empty Cradles (page 132,133,134) regarding Fairbridge Canada are shameful and untrue:

"In all I interviewed about forty people throughout Canada. Most of the children sent to Canada were now in their seventies and eighties."

"Canada was immensely sad for me because it represented a generation of people I knew I could do little to help."

"I told them what had happened in Australia after the second world war and how many children were involved."

"These people touched my heart, and helped me make my decision, I decided I would immediately focus my attention there."

"Before I flew back to England I caught the car ferry and drove to Duncan looking for Fairbridge Farm School."

"There was nobody at the Farm in truth I could see little except a small wooden chapel surrounded by trees."

"When I paid a visit I could hear the sound of children singing as it seeped through the floor of that little wooden chapel that is still active today".

There lies the shame of Margaret Humphreys very poor research. The lady could have easily visited the Archives in Victoria or looked up Fairbridge Canada on the internet which would have provided contact. Many Fairbridge child migrants were not old unless Margaret consider people in their 50's to be old. Humphreys listened to aging home children with not one word of speaking to a Fairbridge Canada child migrants. The home children program was a different child migrant program from the migrant children shipped and placed in the Canadian Fairbridge Farm School. My brother Joe and three sisters were shipped to Pinjarra Western Australia Fairbridge Farm School and surely one of them mentioned a brother that was shipped to Fairbridge Canada in 1947 at age 8. Margaret did visit Fairbridge Canada to attend a reunion of former migrant children, whom attended that little chapel in the trees. Second visit was too late in my opinion to show two faced compassion for kids she abandoned, the damage was done on her first visit.

* * *

After receiving the book from Derek, my nephew Peter, his mum (my sister Janet), and her man Bill came to pick us up and we were on our way to Peter's house – again, on the wrong side of the road. Peter drove a full-size station wagon, with lots of room for five adults and our luggage. There was a strange iron rack mounted by the front bumper of the wagon. Peter informed us that it was a 'roo rack'. I thought, *What the hell is a rue rack?* Peter said it was to protect the vehicle from damage if you ran into a kangaroo, and apparently that happened quite often in Australia. The West Australian scenery was extremely beautiful and had the Indian Ocean at the back door. The geography was very different than what we were used to. Back home we had mountains and rivers to cross. Tunnels had to blast through solid rock and bridges to be built over raging rivers. I thought to myself, "Yes, Australia appears beautiful, but my home British Columbia, Canada is absolutely gorgeous." We noticed many homes were made of brick, along with fences and just about everything else.

We arrived at Peter's house, about a forty-minute drive from Perth. It was a neat, typical suburban home in a new subdivision. After getting settled in, Peter showed us around his home, which was very nice. Their toilet was in a separate room from the main bathroom and it had long and short flush buttons to conserve water. Sheryl found it hard to believe the kitchen sink did not face a window, and there were no cupboards above the countertop or refrigerator area. Their homes weren't bright like our home, and their power system was very different. My sister, Janet, and Bill had to go out for the day as Bill had to see the eye doctor. My sisters were fighting over me. Oh well, at least I felt popular, so far. We spent a fine day with Peter. We spent time at a nature park and got to see koala bears, wild parrots, and kangaroos in their natural habitat. We drove to Kings Park, which overlooked the city of Perth and the Swan River. The trees, shrubbery, and even the grass was different from ours – it felt like another world. We ended the day in a casino, broke even, and Peter drove parallel to the Indian Ocean on our way back to his home. Jan and Bill were back, and we shot the breeze till almost midnight. We had a wonderful day, and now it was time to sleep.

The next morning I tried to send an e-mail to Rita, our good girl at my place of work back home. I am still learning, so it took a while to get the message ready. Peter checked it over and sent the message for me, then we all headed out for breakfast. Sheryl ordered our coffee black, but it came with cream. *Apparently, to get a black coffee you ask for a 'long black', don't ask me why.* Peter drove us to my sister Margaret's near Perth, where we met more relatives. I took a box of Aussie beer that we enjoyed, along with a lovely visit with my sister and part of her family. The hours flew by and we joined up with Peter, Bill, and Janet again. We went to a beautiful pub overlooking the ocean where we met more of Peter's friends. I enjoyed some fish and chips, a couple of beer, and listened to local entertainment. We phoned Mary to see how things were going at home. Mary put the phone to Nicki's ear (the dog) and reported the response was hilarious and that everything was well. Over the next few days, we took in some more tourist activities. We visited a huge marketplace, where two Aboriginals were playing a huge wooden pipe that Bill said was called a 'didgeridoo'. It was painted in a way that told of their culture and reminded me of the Native Indians at home. One morning, I got to watch a crayfish trawler unload the catch of the day (Western Rock Lobster). Then we were off to Freemantle, a deep seaport about thirty miles from Perth, where we saw Captain Cook's ship, *The Endeavor*. We also did the tour of the Freemantle Prison. To look at the gallows where men were hung by the neck was no thrill for us, nor to hear from the guide that a guy had gotten years for stealing two loaves of bread. The girls were not enjoying the tour, so we got out of there. We also took a little ferryboat across Swan River to south Perth and walked to the Zoo. What a magnificent place to spend a few hours. Black swans and animals we had only seen before on television. This experience was unbelievable, and I was happy Bill got it down on video.

Bill and I went to the West Australian Aviation Museum. We both enjoyed the history of flight and marveled at some of the old aircraft. We spent several hours there as it was an excellent display. One evening, we went to a restaurant called the Sizzler – unbelievable food and choices. I could feel the pounds accumulating on my frame and I was thanking God that Canada had no Sizzler restaurants. Afterwards, we went to a shopping mall where I pushed Bill around in a wheelchair. He was not crippled, but rivaled Mr. Bean's comedic talent when he popped out of it, causing people to look on in total amazement. A more serious visit was to the Fairbridge Farm School in Pinjarra, West Australia, about seventy miles north of Perth. This is where the British sent my brother and sisters with hundreds of other kids after the Second World War was over. I was told by my new-found family that it had not been a good experience, and I assured them all that I knew the feeling. The only good thing that came to my mind after checking this place out, was *Thank you God for sending me to Canada*. I might have thought different as a child, but looking at this God-forsaken hole, I knew I had received the best of two evils. It was hot and forlorn. I imagined I could hear my family pleading for help, or at least some love. I snapped back into reality and tears tried to force their way out, but some power always held them back. I had to leave this 'Australian Auschwitz'. The only thing not to be seen were the ovens and the pain on tiny faces. My sister Margaret 'spit the dummy'. Her memories probably triggered a lot of emotion and anger at the rotten life she was served there. We left and her sadness subsided for another day.

On June 1st, we went to visit an eighty-year-old man by the name of Ray Jaechile, who was my deceased sister's husband. Bill drove. We pulled into a driveway, and the house number was 10 Duffy Road. Janet exclaimed that we had arrived, and I felt my heart race. I led our parade up the sidewalk towards the front door of the residence and noticed a young woman through the front room window. She headed in the direction of the door and I thought she must be my niece, and I said so when she opened the door. By the young lady's bewildered look, I quickly filled in a few blanks. Then she smiled and gave us directions – Ray was her neighbor and lived across the road at 9 Duffy Road. It was then I realized that my sister Janet had very little contact, if any, with other family members. This sent alarm bells ringing, and I wondered why. Visiting with Ray turned out to be excellent. He told me about my sister Beryl and his love for her, and the boy and girl that they had together.

We all drove to Pinaroo Park, my sister's final resting place. It was a beautiful place and I enjoyed talking to her for the first time that I could remember. I thought about the letter I received at that cold airbase in Gimli, Manitoba in 1958. Tears came to my eyes as I thought "God, I turned my back on my own sister". As I walked alone, kangaroos were openly eating fresh cut flowers that people had placed for their loved ones who had gone before them. Even with the sadness that flooded my heart, I thought how the kangaroos had the same mission on earth as mine, and that was to survive. We had more family to meet at my brother Joe's place – my nieces, Tara and Rebecca, as well as Tara's husband Malcolm and Beck's fiancé Joseph. It was so great to be reunited, and what a party we had. A surge of sadness ripped through my body, and I fought quickly to gain control of these new emotions that I never knew existed. *This must be the 'family thing'*, I thought. I was dealing with feelings different from anything I had ever experienced in my entire life. Maybe, *blood is thicker than water?*

The next day, we drove to the city of Bunbury where Janet and Bill resided. The trip took about two-and-a-half hours. It was a beautiful drive southwest of Perth, with the Indian Ocean never far away. Janet's home was small, but like a dollhouse, and the backyard was unique. I was looking at twenty-eight wild parrots, called Grey Galahs. I had just counted them when some other parrots landed that were called Twenty Eights. This amused me. The palm trees and lemon trees were unbelievable to a tourist like me and I could not get over the color of a simple thing like road gravel, sort of a red clay texture. Trees and foliage were totally different than back home, and I wondered how they survived with limited water. One type of tree that was called 'Blackboy' was due for a name change. Over the next couple of days, I would meet more relatives. My niece Jenny and husband Mic, and her brothers Mike and Robbie, treated us royally. I wished for more time with them, but the clock was ticking. We stayed at Joe and Diane's for a couple of days. It was so much fun to be with them, even for a short time. Joe took us for a drive away from the city and up through the hills, certainly not mountains as Joe would have us believe.

We checked out the City of Perth dam and water reservoir. It was down to seventeen percent capacity we were told. I thought of all the water in the lakes and streams back home and realized how we took our water for granted. On our last morning everyone was up early, except for Janet. Peter had left for work extremely early and would meet us for a pre-arranged lunch. Bill and I decided to shoot a game of pool, and I asked him if Janet was all right. I just felt like something was off, and Janet had been acting strangely as I had noted from day one. Bill offered no reply. Three days before, I had woken up to a blood-stained pillow with no reasonable explanation. Never in my lifetime had I had a nosebleed for no reason, and there was no sign of one now. I was confused, as I had no nicks, scratches, or cuts from shaving either. I thought of a couple other nights when I had woken in the early hours (between 3 and 4 am) to a very strange sound. I woke Sheryl to listen one time, and finally decided to peek out the bedroom door. Much to my amazement, it was the sound of a mop being swished back and forth across the floor by Janet. I asked her why she was doing this at such strange hours, and she replied, "To keep the dust down, as Peter does not have the floors finished in this new home". *Odd,* I thought, but *Oh well! Different strokes for different folks.*

Janet finally made her presence known that morning, and by her body language I could tell she was not happy. I asked her if she was feeling 'crook', as they say, and she blurted out some unintelligible words in an angry manner. I asked her again, "What's wrong, Janet?" and as I tried to approach her, she went ballistic. This, I realized, was called 'spitting the dummy', and it was terrible. Janet went on a rant, yelling that we did not *have* to leave. Then she began screaming about the English girl, Pat, not being our real sister. A handful of other hurtful and hateful things spewed out of her mouth. My wife Sheryl was quite shaken and, with tears in her eyes, she begged Janet to tell us why she was so upset. Janet then called Sheryl a *bitch*, and that did it for me! I advised Janet that she had met her opponent in me, her younger brother, and I lost my composure. I asked Bill one more time to help me understand what was wrong. I told Janet that nobody treats my wife that way. I then proceeded to rattle her, and I do believe she had never seen her own fury defeated like the one confronting her. Janet screamed at Bill to pack quickly, so they could leave for home and Sheryl and I could fend for ourselves in a country we were not familiar with at all. Little Bill, who we gave the nickname 'Mr. Bean', looked terrified, and obeyed her command immediately. I was devastated, but in control. I advised Janet never to come to our country, Canada, or to bother us again. My mind was on high alert, and we needed a new plan to get to our flight out of Perth today. A taxi to the airport would be our last resort. I thought of asking Peter. I could not get a hold of Peter, so I phoned my sister-in-law Diana, who in turn got a hold of my brother Joe. Joe made the long journey to where we were just in time to ask Janet what was wrong. He got rewarded by having a door slammed in his face, and a minute later, Janet and Bill drove away. Joe drove us to the airport with Diane and the girls.

My nephew, Peter, joined us for our last lunch together in this 'land down under' and he asked where his mother (Janet) and Bill were. It was difficult to tell him details, but we managed to gently communicate the message of the poisonous words of wrath that had come from Janet. Peter stood strong in disbelief of his mother's actions. I told him that it would be next to impossible to mend the cracks we had intended to heal after a lifetime of being apart. I sincerely felt for her and wondered how many times a heart could be broken. Some other family did not come to lunch, as it was difficult to say goodbye. Boarding the aircraft was emotional, indeed. A picture of my niece Tara remains in my heart as she desperately fought to stop the flow of tears that glistened in the steady rain. My head was swimming with thoughts of anger directed at England, a country that could separate children and exile one sibling to the other side of the world. My eyes were moist, but

I refused to cry, as I remembered my oath I took when I was twelve years old – no more tears, no more religion, and little room for the new word 'love'. It was raining hard as we left the runway and climbed quickly out of sight.

CHAPTER EIGHTEEN: BACK TO LONDON

Rod and my sister, Pat, were there to greet us when we landed in London. Pat informed us that Janet had phoned them and said we had changed our flight plan to Canada and would not be landing in England! I decided Janet probably needed psychiatric help. Fortunately, Pat and Rod did not believe Janet and drove the two hours to Heathrow airport to greet us. Rod drove us north to Birmingham, the city where I was born. I had a different kind of excitement to deal with and looked forward to the adventure. The English countryside was green as could be. One would think it would be all worn out after all the centuries, crusades, and wars it had endured. Pat and Rod lived in a typical English house, like you would see in a movie – lots of bricks and very quaint. We met their four daughters who ranged in age from fourteen, to thirty years old. It was nice to be accepted by them all.

Pat was the sister that was adopted out at seven months old to an English couple, whom she said treated her poorly. When they passed away, Pat launched her own search to find out who she really was, and some things fell into place. Rod stood by Pat in her search, and through their efforts they found things out that would curl your hair. They had been to Australia twice, and I did wonder about that. *Why had they not inquired about a visit to Canada?* I pondered. Pat had absolutely no resemblance to the Isherwoods in Australia, or myself. There was a lot more to this puzzle, as it would unfold.

We had met a lady by the name of Grace Baker, in Australia. Grace was in her seventies and very close to our mother when she had lived in England. Pat Murtagh was the spitting image of Grace when we compared pictures, and the resemblance was uncanny when we finally met Pat. I bit my tongue and filed it under *What happened?* One story suggests that Grace Baker, being so young, had Pat out of wedlock in post-war England and Elsie Isherwood (my mother) saved Grace by claiming the child was her own. We had a good chat session that evening, but fatigue had me beat and my body ached for sleep. Some Old English fish and chips, a hot shower, and I was soon fast asleep in loo loo land, oblivious to my strange surroundings. The next day was pleasant, as we swapped stories and memories of the past. We all went to a local pub later in the day and listened to karaoke (English style!). I could not get the picture of this lady with the name Grace Baker out of my mind. Grace was old enough to be Pat's mother, and she was in that English circle long ago. There was so much on my plate, I had become emotionally and mentally tired on this journey.

I decided to make the best of the trip, and sort out all of these thoughts later. Rod certainly knew England well and showed us so much in such little time. Sheryl and Pat got along well and chatted constantly. Another sunny day and we were off to a place called Lichfield, about 25 miles away. Lorna, the youngest daughter had joined us, and we found her to be so delightful. Approaching Lichfield, we could see three spheres that seemed to reach the clouds. Getting closer we could see the church they belonged to which took one's breath away. We were told it had been constructed in the year 1222 and was like no other in the world. To tour the inside was like stepping back in time as your imagination could form your own pictures and bring back the sounds from so long ago. It was ever so easy for anyone to spend hours going through this magnificent, historic village. An added surprise was a parade with floats and marching bands with plenty of precision and color. I got to shake hands with the Sheriff of Lichfield, and I glimpsed back to the story of Robin Hood and King Richard, the Lion Hearted.

The girls decided to look through the quaint shops after feasting off a modern McDonalds menu. Sheryl bought a stuffed talking bird that still brings much laughter. After a very nice time and many questions later, we headed back to the house. Later, son in-law Nigel and wife Nicola came for a visit and a few beers. The television was turned on and we watched a splendid soccer match between England and Germany. This reminded me of my young days when I lived and breathed soccer. Sheryl did not share my enthusiasm with contact sports, including hockey. While we watched soccer, her time was spent talking on the phone to our people back home. She had never done this kind of international travel and was enjoying it immensely. Come to think about it, neither had I under my own steam. There was never a dull moment and I wished things could be the way they were presented to me. At this point I was relying heavily on others to prove and show me the way. I drifted off in a peaceful sleep, thinking of the progress made, be it right or wrong. The next morning, we received a phone call from a Birmingham newspaper and a time was agreed upon to meet. While we waited, I sifted through a pile of documents that Rod and Pat had acquired. What I read could not be confirmed by me, but I did notice the many times Middlemore Homes and the Cadbury family names were mentioned. The agreed time passed, and we made a call to the newspaper but got no satisfactory reply as to the reporters where abouts. Rod mentioned a drive to Cadbury Chocolate factory for a look, as it was renown around the world. Indeed, it was impressive, and I could see it employed a lot of people. We did not get a tour of the place as hoped but did eat many assorted chocolates. After touring more hamlets along winding roads and country lanes it was time for a rest.

Rod pulled into an English Legion that made Sheryl's day. Stating that she was President and a lifetime member of Branch Number 265 Royal Canadian Legion brought immediate friendship. Free beer followed and a deal was made to exchange mementos between the two Legions. Evening came and we treated Rod, Pat, and family to a fine meal in a beautiful pub named Mill Pond. I decided not to look at weigh scales till I got home. Never did hear from the reporter or the local Member of Parliament.

It was 30 Celsius with clear blue sky. One day left and the oldest girl Samantha and her man Jamie had invited us to a barbecue. They owned a caravan that we call a travel trailer and were camped in a park some twenty miles away. The drive there was nice, away from the battle of the motorways. I thought how brave people were towing their caravans over such narrow and winding roads. The food was excellent, followed by a good walk in the park. They asked many questions about Canada and our lifestyle in such a young country. They had seen pictures of huge mountain ranges and forests that we confirmed to be true. All of a sudden there was a roar overhead and a sight to behold appeared like magic. We were treated to low flying squadrons of Skyhawk fighter jets heading to their airbase. I could read the aircraft number on the fuselage even at that speed. My grandson Jimmy who is an air cadet would have been thrilled to witness that. We said some good-byes and were on the road again.

The time has arrived, and we must pack. A pleasant evening was had by all but tomorrow would arrive quickly and reality will reappear. Today we would fly back to Canada. The ride to Heathrow Airport from Birmingham was a happy one, but the stillness would take over and somber thoughts entered my head. Like, how did we manage to crowd so much fun and chatter into four days? We never did get to see my three uncles and aunts, cousins, nephews, or nieces. We will wait for another day and God willing, we shall return. Arriving at the Airport we checked in and now had time for a bite to eat. We had just sat down with our soup and a photographer, reporter introduced himself. First thing you know he is taking pictures and making notes and promises of things to come. Unbelievable he exclaimed! How did this happen, incredible, amazing! Nice flow of adjectives but bottom line, we never heard from him again. I was accustomed to this rejection and was glad I warned him of our plight and advised him the story would go nowhere.

Heathrow Terminal was swarming with people trying to get a flight. Apparently, there was a computer problem at Gatwick Airport some miles away that allowed very little movement of Aircraft, and Heathrow was taking up some slack. The 747 Jumbo was loaded to capacity, but the powerful Rolls Royce engines thundered down the runway and poof, we left the ground for the friendly skies and Canada. The flight was smooth but cramped, cabin crew were excellent all the way and I felt like a veteran traveler. I looked down over Iceland and thought of man on the moon, as it appeared man had lots to explore right here on earth. The view was spectacular from this altitude and I marveled at the technology that kept this huge bird in the sky. The hours slipped by and I was now looking down on the Canadian Rocky Mountain Range. It just didn't get any better than this and I secretly thought that British Columbia was the most beautiful place on earth, at least from the air.

Time could not go by quick enough now as the aircraft started descending over the Fraser Valley that was our home. We could see the mighty Fraser River winding its way like a ribbon to eventually end up in the Pacific Ocean. The Fraser was the only tidal river I was aware of. The river was world renown for the salmon that returned from the Sea and navigated this treacherous uphill battle to reach their spawning grounds where they had got their very beginning. Man have since built fish ladders to help them up and over many man-made obstacles, such as the damns that generate electrical power. At times, some tributaries were completely diverted for highway construction or logging. The fishing industry has really suffered at the hands of man but then so has the forestry, or for that matter, most things to do with nature. As I looked down, I wondered why ordinary folk understood the environment problems so well and yet, were powerless to act. The ones we elected to look after the peoples' land continue to screw things up. They forget quickly who put them there and tend to think the dollar bill will correct all the ills man has thrown at mother nature. Anyway, that is another story to be told another day. Seat belt sign was on and we began our final approach to Vancouver International Airport. The landing was smooth as silk. I thought, "God, we had almost flown around the world.

We cleared customs and the rest of the Airport stuff and quickly spotted Sheryl's sister Margaret and her husband Donald who came to greet us and drive us home. After lots of chatter and many questions later we ended up where our own car was stored. We were extremely tired now and drove the remaining ten miles to our home. As we pulled in the driveway our dog Nikita was overjoyed. I said to Sheryl, if she wags her little stump tail much harder her bum will fall off! I now know what is meant by the words "Home Sweet Home", going away and returning to your own bed. This trip is over and most appreciated; but in reality, it could turn out to be the saddest part of my entire life. Words like "what you don't know won't hurt you". If this is true then the system has hurt me one more time. It is a long chain with many broken links that God himself is incapable of repairing, not to mention the emptiness that is forever in my heart. No, I will never forgive England or the people responsible, never ever.

CHAPTER NINETEEN: PAT, 2001

After meeting a long-lost sister (half-sister? Full? I am still not sure), Pat, and her lovely family in England, another dream was shattered. Our visit lasted a lousy four days, during which we tried to figure out who was who in the Isherwood/Baker family. Pat and her husband, Rod, spent endless hours trying to piece the jigsaw of her young life together. Finally, her dream was becoming reality and for the first time in her life she was meeting her real brothers and sisters too. Pat and Rod had been to Australia and met a lot of the family that had been sent there fifty years prior to their arrival. In May 2000, my wife Sheryl and I flew to England where Pat and Rod would join us on the long flight to Australia to have a gala reunion. Pat got ill and was unable to make the trip, so Sheryl and I carried on alone.

When we got back to England, Pat's illness was downplayed and thought to be the flu. We shared a joyful, short time together. Back in Canada, we kept in touch by telephone and e-mail, and planned for a future get together. In April 2001, we received a dreaded phone call from Rod – Pat had passed away and her funeral would take place on April 12, 2001. I have never felt such a feeling of disbelief. A cloud of sadness came over me and I thought *Is there a God?* Powers that be had ripped this family apart again. I could not go to England as I was getting medical testing myself and there was too much stress involved. Rod had known Pat's illness was more severe but had bravely kept it away from family. A lot of the answers Pat had tried to find about our past will not go unchallenged, as her family will champion the cause.

CHAPTER TWENTY: PIER 21

I was looking through the television guide and decided to watch a documentary on the History Channel titled Pier 21. You could not imagine my surprise when a picture of the troop ship *Aquitania* appeared on the television screen. The ship I sailed on across the North Atlantic Ocean to Halifax, Nova Scotia Canada. After five days crossing the sometimes-unforgiving sea, the *Aquitania* docked at pier 21, May 25th, 1947. My gosh I thought, this is truly exciting. They claim that everything that went through Pier 21 was on micro- film and that meant information was there waiting for me.

A lot was said about English War Brides that landed and were given Canadian Citizenship as soon as they were married. The mention of 1500 soldiers that disembarked brought on a memory of soldiers giving us small fry chocolate bars on the voyage across the ocean. I decided to buy and learn the computer and did so with vengeance. E-mail became very important to my well-being and proved to be a great asset. The girls where I work are incredibly patient helping me to reach my goal and shall never be forgotten. I was talking by phone to a lady at the Jewish Society in the City of Vancouver. We were swapping war stories when I asked if she was familiar with Pier 21. Just like that I had the e-mail address for Pier 21 and on October 27, 2000 I sent my first e-mail to whoever. All I could do now is wait, but this time it was not long as a reply came within the hour. It came from a Librarian, Carrie-Ann, at Pier 21 Halifax Nova Scotia. She explained they were ahead four hours in time and their day was over. She promised to get back with more detail and in the meantime said to enjoy the picture of the ship *Aquitania*, as it appeared when I was aboard fifty-three years ago. My heart was pounding, at last help was here, so I thought. The picture is now the wallpaper on my PC, the third largest troop ship and the most rat infested in the fleet. I would ask if that included twenty-eight rug rats and would get a very negative answer. No mention of children! Carrie-Ann kept her word, replying that no record of the *Aquitania* calling in May of 1947 was to be found. I faxed a copy of the landed immigrant card and a copy of the young boarding party just prior to leaving England. Magically, another source confirmed that the Ship called twice that month with no mention of children on board. Are you confused yet? I am.

Carrie-Ann tried desperately to help but as always, the trail of the 28 kids cooled down so much that people would give up in total frustration. On December 15, 2000 Carrie-Ann said, "I am stumped". I thanked Carrie-Ann as though it was to be a final farewell and I prepared to charter a new course, as I knew not to give up. Truly my very being, heart, and soul have been through many wringers. Why there is no help is beyond comprehension.

It is now March 2001; I have emailed several times to Carrie-Ann as she did say to write anytime. It seems they might have vacated the premises or been told to shut up on this historic matter. "Hate" is a bad word but I now allow it in my vocabulary. Desperately, I asked the Archives in Victoria to conduct another search for my records as another boy now grown had received his in 1992. I received the same old answer, negative on my existence for years 1947 to 1955. Since this crusade was started, I have spoken with four kids that were part of the group of twenty-eight, and they were two sets of brothers who reported a lot of sadness in their younger lives. Stories that are identical in hardships and abuse, sexual and physical. The nonexistent love or hugs and the constant working your little fingers to the bone. As a mere child not belonging to anyone or anything, where my greatest love was for a dog named Woolly, whom I shared with a couple of hundred other kids as the dog loved us all. As I said to Carrie-Ann, "things are more silent than the guns of "Naverone". Other people who question the wisdom of my pursuit to know the truth I would tell them, "When you go home tonight and your children are gone forever never to be seen again, simply to say, don't worry about it" no big deal is it? Or when war is declared, and you have lost everything like family and all possessions. Your cities and countryside are under constant attack and you are frightened to death, don't worry about it. Maybe think about the good people that suffered and gave their lives so you could breathe fresh air. Don't worry about it, the fresh air is disappearing and when it does, it will affect those other smart people along with the common person. We can finally tell them, "Don't worry about it" your money and stature can't help you.

A message came on March 21, 2001, from Carrie-Ann, Librarian at Pier 21 Halifax, Nova Scotia. The last communication from her was on December 15, 2000, with words I did not want to hear, "I am stumped". I thought I would never hear from her again. Her email informed me that she had found an article in the Gazette titled, *Waifs:*

The Fairbridge Society in British Columbia, 1931- 1951. The name below the title snapped me to full attention. It was the name of an archivist with the provincial Archives of British Columbia. I had previously met this man in the 90's. For several hours we had talked extensively in a licensed establishment overlooking the Nanaimo harbor on Vancouver Island. The things I thought he could help me with warmed my heart along with the booze. He got me hook, line, and sinker. I paid the bar bill, thanked him ever so much, and never heard from him again. I had tried to phone him but as usual, to no avail.

This archivist did give me a refresher course in the word trust. Something he obviously lacked and was out for his own material gain. I started digging into my own basket of knowledge and the first thought staring at me were the words "Live and learn", "There is a sucker born every minute", and "Don't sweat the small stuff". These are but a few of the truest sayings ever spoken. To this man, wherever you are, thanks again for nothing! The one thing the Gazette said was, "Newspapers across the country lavished attention on the school in heart-warming accounts of "manly young lads" and "bonny lasses". [6] Daily life at the farm was chronicled along with the distinguished visitors that came to view us in this Children's Zoo, free of charge. The irony is they stumbled over each other to take credit when in fact they were ruining a lot of young lives, as the future would unfold with the true story of the migrant children. As usual, the truth is still untold, and I still do not exist after all this attention Fairbridge received. Probably no room in the newspapers to write about the kids, as it must have been extremely difficult finding space for all those pompous people. I survived the entire Second World War from start to finish and then you decide to kidnap and separate me from my family till the end of time. Gee! Thanks a lot.

Mr. Logan, the principal of Fairbridge Farm School helped put me in an orbit so extreme that I can never re-enter the life on earth that God had meant for me to have with my own family. That life was many light years in the past. I wish we could have shared a stale bread, cheese, and dandelion sandwich with you all. However, I would never wish for another to experience the sexual acts the older boys made us perform.

---

6. Dunae, Patrick. "Waifs: The Fairbridge Society in B.C., 1931–1951." *Social History* 219, no. 42 (November 1988): page 237.

Why does it feel as though none of you gave a shit about us children. Face reality, you all came before the kid's interest and the same applies to this day. As the English used to say, "Good Riddance to Bad Rubbish".

I can now say that to them, along with, there is another crack in your Empire. You are running low on British White Stock from what the world sees, as the Brit's said so many years ago. Oh well! maybe you would like to buy us back from Canada and start another crusade.

Today is March 25, 2001

The weather has been record setting in British Columbia this past winter. Very little snowfall on the lower mainland and Fraser Valley area where I live. Daffodils, tulips, and crocus bulbs are up and reaching for the sun but the mountains that surround us with snow-capped peaks defy anything to top their natural beauty. I think of Agnes, three thousand miles east of BC in the province of Ontario where winter rages on. Agnes had phoned me back in January and seemed quite excited. Agnes told me that there was a trip to England being offered, as there were many family members that I had never met and was unaware of. At first, I was cautiously optimistic, and I wondered if I could stand the strain and emotional tension of going back to yesteryear again. My wife and I decided it was the only way to seek some kind of reckoning with the past, but I would never forgive what happened to me. The other side of the coin is we are getting older and time stands still for no man. Agnes phoned again to confirm this trip would happen. The only thing pending was how to prove my English uncles were my mother's brothers.

Confusion and stress were banging on my door again. Then I remembered my sister Margaret in Australia had sent me a copy of my mum and dad's marriage certificate. It showed mother's maiden name as Allen and it showed her brother's surname Allen, as a witness to the marriage. Yikes! The certificate is dated nineteen thirty-two and I was nowhere in sight. I faxed this information to Agnes in Ottawa and thought, why put the onus on me? I was the one abducted. I asked Agnes to see if her English counterpart could help me research over in England and then it dawned on me. Why did England not simply phone my uncles? As I write this down, I am still waiting to hear from Agnes. In the meantime, I have sent a letter to the House of Commons,

England, thanking them for not answering my last letter. It is very difficult to put down anything nice about such a rude group of people. I wonder what the ordinary English folk would think if they knew the absolute truth as to what the government did to English babies.

I mailed a letter to the Australian Prime Minister to let him know the truth about the Canadian part of Margaret Humphrey's book titled "Empty Cradles". I have never read such a load of bull, and that lady was another one that did not have the gumption or decency to reply to my quest for the truth. Margaret became a big part of my inspiration to get out a book of truth from a Canadian Migrants point of view. Like I say, "if you have not done the walk, do not do the talk". This advice seems reasonable to most folk. If I should get a reply from whomever I shall be ecstatic, but for now I will not hold my breath.

Agnes phoned on March 27, 2001 to confirm that the trip to the UK was a green light. Agnes was informed there are dozens of my kin anxious to meet their lone ranger Canadian. If people realized how difficult it is to meet your own family for a few hours out of a lifetime, and to see how you differ in culture is unbelievable. I am damned if I do and damned if I don't, it's like being stuck between a rock and a hard place. To be extremely happy and sad at the same time is most unusual. Derek is a social worker for the Child Migrant Trust that is based in England. The director of the trust, "Margaret Humphreys" was the author of the book Empty Cradles. The book tells many untruths concerning Child Migrants in Canada. I am living proof of her lack of research and the feeble attempt to find the truth. It is somebody's duty to write the truth on this sad part of history.

The Letter:

Derek: I received your letter and am responding to a couple of things that bug me.

1. I don't know if it was a clerical error or deliberate sending me to Canada. I choose deliberate, errors of this magnitude could have been corrected easily.

2. You say I was unclear about who was responsible for this crime. Stop and think, how old I was and how the adults invited me to speak my mind (Never). Give me a break and let's use common sense.

3. I said I would enjoy reading Empty Cradles before a page had been opened. My wildest dreams would not anticipate what lay in wait between the covers especially the Canadian report, it was sad. I sent a letter to the House of Commons England seeking help and I was referred to Miss Chris Corrigan Section Head Department of Health. A Dr. John Benger sent this information on behalf of Mr. David Hinchcliffe chairman of the Health Committee.

I did as he instructed and sent more than one letter. As usual, I am waiting for a reply, I won't hold my breath.

4. The book Empty Cradles said it all, the trust did not work hard in Canada, if it had we would not be corresponding in this manner.

5. David Lorente, Home Children Canada has met Margaret Humphreys and has been in touch with me. The sad part nobody seems to understand, we were not home children. Also, it is Pier 21 I referred to not 28. The staff there find the plight of 28 lost children unbelievable.

The troop ship Aquitania did indeed dump us off at Pier 21 May 25, 1947. Seems everything is on documentaries and microfilm but us little beggars. The classic Oliver Twist could have been written about a kid like me. Another boy that came over with me phoned me last week; we were fast friends when we were incarcerated during the war and Fairbridge in Canada. His memory is better than mine on some of the goings on at Fairbridge. He claims for sure that even his older brother sexually molested us.

This man got his records from the Archives in Victoria British Columbia of his young years. The same people who say I don't exist. Can people not see my total frustration? GOD would even say, enough is enough, help him and don't hinder as they are doing. The British punished me to eternity. What did I do wrong that you desperately try to run and hide from?

The International Association of former Child Migrants and their Families got in touch. The President Norman Johnston and I had a pleasant talk on the phone about different things and class action lawsuits. Interesting for the Australians but under careful consideration I have decided to go it alone. My situation is unique, and I shall carry on without your help. The American talk show is not that far off, and the truth shall rule. My Brother Joseph's youngest girl is to be married in March 2001 and I thought how great if I could surprise her at her wedding. That is until I checked the airfares. It would cost three hundred dollars a day just to be away for ten days.

This is what the British have done and makes no effort to repair the links in our broken chain. The latter is for Margaret Humphreys to see and take it to your friends in England.

One more thing, The British Press tracked "me" down with all the promises and the right words as to what a story they would print. I keep the names handy of several Editors from over there so I can spit on them once in a while. They could never imagine the damage they did to my family and I shall hate them forever. Derek, I have copies of old documents that would curl your hair. The lies that were swapped back and forth, even when I was in my twenties, is unbelievable.

The trust did not unite my family. We did it on our own, with a lot of luck. Uniting is not always the pleasant thing that people assume it is. It can buy you more emotional hardship than a lot of folks could bear. I often think of an elastic band – you can stretch it or stretch it till it breaks. Our band is broken forever, thanks again to the British high rollers. I am still waiting after many years for someone to tell me who Mrs. Wilburforce was?

Old document says she was on some welfare committee during and after the war years. It goes on to say the lady took a special interest in the Isherwood family and had come to Canada and seen Tommy. Tommy does not remember seeing her.

Happy New Year,
Regards

Tom Isherwood

$$* * *$$

July 20, 2001

Gosh, try to imagine my surprise when I checked my email on July 20, 2001. Kathy Tomlinson, a producer for the Canadian Broadcasting Corporation was willing to get in touch concerning the saga of British Child Migrants sent to Canada after the war was long over. I became truly excited at the thought of finally getting professional help to try to unravel the sad mystery from the past. Maybe now the English will open up the doors that have concealed their evil deeds against British babies, cast from the Island and their families till the end of time. I made contact with Kathy immediately, and July 23, 2001 we met at my home and a new journey began.

My wife Sheryl had to reign me in once in a while as I tried to convey over sixty years of knowledge and memory to Kathy in one breath. I collected some composure but at times, rattled on like a Mode T- Ford on a gravel road. Kathy was easy to relate to and the three of us got through a lovely day. The ultimate surprise came when Kathy said, "What do you think of having company on the trip to the UK". No sooner said than done, a seat change called for to allow us to sit together as Sheryl and I were already booked to fly Air Canada on a 747-400 Jumbo Jet. A simple phone call took care of the seat change. Man, my mind was working overtime and it seemed like a dream. Another surprise came in the mail from the honourable Sheila Copps, Minister of Canadian Heritage and the Historic Sites and Monuments Board of Canada. She invited me to the unveiling of a plaque commemorating the national historic significance of Home Children.

The ceremony would take place in the province of Ontario, about three thousand miles away from the province of British Columbia where I live. This is the strange part, 55yrs being in Canada and this is the first time I have had contact on this so-called historic event. I find it amusing, as there is no record of my arrival on the ship *Aquitania* May 25, 1947 at the historic Pier 21 in the city of Halifax, province of Nova Scotia. In fact, I have a document from Immigration Canada that claims no records can be found as to me being in this country. No records exist in the National or British Columbia Archives of my early years from 1947 to 1955. I emailed MP Sheila Copps on September 13, 2000 desperately seeking some kind of help. My message was read and went unanswered, and I have the copy of my email to prove it. Politicians only surface to fill their own need for glory and media opportunities.

I would love to be there for several reasons. First, how many of you home children gathered at the plaque unveiling came to Canada after the Second World War. I mentioned that I did every day of the War with perfect attendance. Immigration charged two hundred dollars for the pleasure of becoming a citizen of a country where I never had a choice or say in being here. The Prime Minister at the time, "McKenzie King" granted British so-called War Brides, many of them in a family way, Citizenship as soon as they arrived in Canada and were married to their lovers. Some of them arrived on the troop ship *Aquitania*, according to a documentary on the Historic Pier 21. No mention or pictures of 28 little British kids being processed on May 25, 1947 and transported to a farm for the under privileged on Vancouver Island, British Columbia. We were Oliver Twist indeed and worked our fingers to the bone and ate off tin dishes. I thank you for that. I personally wish to thank the Government of England and Canada for agreeing to separate me from a large family and change my religion to suit the needs of the day. The fires of hell cannot stomach the thoughts of what people did to my family and me. Your plaque does not put out the fire in my heart.

CHAPTER TWENTY-ONE: CBC

August 14, 2001 arrived quickly, and I helped my wife Sheryl, packing and preparing for possibly the most informative trip of my lifetime. For some reason, the Canadian Broadcasting Corporation had managed to pry open doors to vaults that contained what surely must be dusty documents of my childhood. Over six decades have passed and this will be the first time my eyes will look into a window from so long ago. My feelings are hard for me to describe, as I will be meeting Uncles, Aunts, and many cousins I have never met or even heard from in over sixty years of living. I knew it would be hard on my real family and me emotionally. I summoned all my strength, energy, and my survival skills accumulated over my lifetime to prepare me for what lay ahead. If I had only known that you cannot prepare for a thing called love.

Wednesday, August 15 found us on the freeway to Vancouver International Airport. I thought quickly of my daughters, grandsons, my dog Nikita, and the years we had shared together as our own little family. We checked our baggage and met Kathy Tomlinson and Don Scott, the cameraman who had flown in from the province of Alberta, east of British Columbia. Kathy wasted no time and gave us a quick briefing and the production was underway. Dozens of people from around the world looked curiously at us as they made their way about the airport, which is huge. This is completely new to Sheryl and I, but it did not seem too difficult facing the camera. The time came to board the aircraft and it dawned on me that I had not flown with Air Canada, the National airline since it was called T.C.A, or Trans-Canada Airlines. I thought, "My goodness, those were the days of propeller driven flight" and I realized time had ripped by. Some confusion with our seating on flight 3090, but it worked out.

The Jet is roaring down the runway at seven-ten PM, and just like that we are airborne and knifing through the clouds to thirty-three thousand feet. Kathy decided to shoot film on the aircraft. My overhead light that was needed, did not work when I tried the switch. It turned out the switch two rows ahead controlled my light, and we summoned the flight attendant who would log this strange occurrence. People are very curious when they see a camera, and questions and guessing take place. The flight attendant just had to ask what was happening and I could not resist a reply. Without a miscue I told her that I had been notified some months ago that a castle and estate waited for me in Transylvania, as I was a lost Prince and heir to a fortune. To my total amazement she believed this tale and immediately offered her name and phone number and asked to please keep in touch. I let her dwell for a while and savored the moment. On hearing the truth, she called me a name in fun, mind you, and we shared a good laugh. Turned out she lived just a few kilometers from us, and we would phone her on our return. I asked for a drink later on, she informed me to get my own. The aircraft touched down at Heathrow Airport, London England at 11:40 am British time, eight hours ahead of British Columbia, Canada time. The flight took approximately nine hours and it was good to be on the ground.

Heathrow Airport looked the same as we left it just over a year ago. People from all over the world going in more than four different directions, each one sharing a common goal, to go or get back from all corners of the globe. We cleared customs and immigration, pushing our luggage on this neat little cart and making our way to the next level. There was a man holding up a sign that said CBC. Too easy, his name was Michael, and he was the soundman and driver hired by the CBC to get us safely to wherever we might go. More film shot at Heathrow and we loaded Michael's Van to the roof. It was after 1200 PM and we started out on a long drive to Wales, already tired but adrenaline flowing with excitement and curiosity. I had stated early on that tears were hard come by for me and I wondered silently, what might have been. British Motorways appeared loaded to capacity and I mused, so many people driving on the wrong side of the road. Hard to make headway and I thought, never should I grumble at a mere traffic light holding me up at home. Eventually we turned off the motorway and at some point, entered Wales.

The roads were now so narrow and winding it made my eyes open wide. The scenery is indescribable beauty; you have to see it to believe it. On and on we drove, every turn showed us a new picture and we finally entered a small town called Barmouth, situated by the Irish Sea. We all agreed, "breath-taking to say the least" and agreed to check it out when we got settled. At last, the St. David Hotel where we would stay and Michael steered off the narrow road, parked, and stopped to give the engine a well-earned rest. I did not notice how nice our accommodation was until the next day at a very good breakfast. I had slept like Rip Van Winkle once I had counted all the sheep in Wales. Tired as we were, I had phoned my Uncle Dennis to let him pass the word we had arrived safely. After breakfast I phoned for directions. Uncle Dennis said they were only a ten-minute drive away from the hotel. I wrote down the directions and read them back to him. He said we would pass a big blue garage and the very next corner would be my Aunt Sheila in a white T-shirt.

We whistled right by our directions by about eight minutes and immediately turned around. I spotted a blue garage that in our Country is very small, and a lady standing on the corner of a nearby road in a black sweater with her back facing us. We all pondered, when the lady turned around to display a white T-shirt under the black sweater. Auntie had simply got cold waiting for us, so we all had a chuckle. At this moment I met my Auntie Sheila for the first time in my life. The energy from the hugging forced my feelings to take a stronger command. I was not familiar with this kind of attack on my inner fortress. It worked, and my thoughts stopped what appeared to be tears of rain on the way. I felt a great genuine feeling of warmth when I hugged that woman who was my real Aunt.

Family Reunion - Wales

Sheryl and I walked the short distance to my Cousin Eileen's house where I met two uncles, Bert and Dennis for the first time in my life. Uncle Bert would say that he knew me when I was a toddler but obviously it did not register for me. We were told that Aunt Eileen would join us a little later. I met one daughter of Uncle Bert's named Sheila, after her Aunt Sheila. Sheila's girl was named Eileen, after Bert's wife Eileen. This happens when two brothers marry two sisters. I met my cousin Derek and his wife Lucy, who was a real English Bobby and had driven a fair piece to be here for me. It seemed like they had all loved me forever and my brain and mind were doing battle to control this new set of emotions that were strangers to my inner world. I thought, *"God Damn this is hard to do"*. The reunion in Australia, meeting my brothers and sisters had not been this hard on me. Later, I figured my kin in Australia were like me and showed little outward emotion, even though the love was there between us. This part of our family had been raised as a family. They had been together all their lives and being a mite younger had not gone through the horrors of war as I did. I thanked God for that as he had left a little of the once large family intact as a loving unit. Now, for a brief moment in time, I could look in their window and share family love and all their emotion. Things were great and it was like a pleasant fire was burning in my heart. Then my Aunt Eileen arrived, more hugging and my feelings now were out of control as I saw all the tears that surrounded me. The river of tears would not stop the raging fire in my body and I had to escape my family to be alone. I don't believe Samson would have been strong enough to weather this storm. My system failed me and tears started to flow, and I thought of the last time when I was ten years old and made a vow not to cry again. Over fifty years have gone by and the lake was full, waiting for the dam to burst.

I thought my heart would surely explode and my head felt like it was being reconstructed to handle the day. My body felt weak, sad, and happy all at the same time, a strange feeling of peace came over me. I thought of GOD who I believed in when I was little so many years ago. Why did he do this to his children? No one has found the answer, and until then I don't have much faith. My newfound family put on a barbecue fit for a king. My wife Sheryl shared some of her cooking expertise and exchanged recipes and knowledge, and a great time was had by all. It was perfect if there is such a thing, and I thanked Derek's wife Lucy for going the extra mile for us. John Mart, the man of the house showed up from working all day and at first, I thought he was a guest or cousin. John works for a man whose title is Lord Harlee and has an estate in Wales. I kind of thought this Lord stuff had disappeared along with King John and the crusades. I dubbed my new relative Lord John, much to the glee of others.

John had quickly found the bottle of Canadian Whiskey we had got for Uncle Dennis and decided to sample it. Lord John offered me a stiff one which I declined and had a beer instead. When Dennis found out, he quickly hid his prize whiskey elsewhere, which added to the merriment. I found myself with the others, pointing out similarities that our bodies shared from tip to toe. It was amazing and the warm buzz in my heart had settled down and seemed like we had been together many times. Damn, I felt so proud to be with them, and knowing they had all done well in their chosen lives was delightful. I have never witnessed a closer loving family and now I am part of it from a very distant land. For this I shall always feel sad when I think of what should have been, but I am also very proud of the Canadian family that I helped create and my wife's side of the family that truly accepted me almost forty years ago.

Wales

Darkness came with the evening and we all walked to a very quaint British pub. My uncles had arranged a private room to do some work with CBC and to have a few beers. We left the pub around midnight no worse for the wear. I filed a very fond memory of a once in a lifetime very special day. Not too many people in this world can share this kind of experience, and I thank God they don't have too. Back at the Hotel and looking forward to pleasant dreams about our day, gone by like a rush of wind. Saturday morning, August 18, 2001 had arrived. I lay in bed trying to evaluate what has taken place and how it will change my life forever. I asked myself, "Is it a good thing or a bad thing to reunite for such a small-time frame". A blink of an eye in over sixty years. Is the stone better being left unturned, or open this window of opportunity and pray that all goes well. The doors of sadness keep opening and closing like broken window shutters, flapping back and forth in a violent windstorm. It is a case of love versus sadness and when I go back to my foreign home; I shall try to go with distant love and put my emotional breakdown to rest one more time.

I got up at 8 am, shaved, showered, and met camera crew for a splendid English breakfast. The weather has really changed and is raining hard. There was a golf tournament planned and golfers. They had a gung-ho attitude and I wished them luck. Sheryl and I decided to have a leisurely day and to charge the emotional batteries. We met Camera crew and off again to John and Eileen's, another splendid visit. Kathy was now filming our good-byes and I felt a deep pit forming in my stomach. I knew this live dream was breaking up and part of me was heading back to loneliness. My brain had already ordered reconstruction of my thought shields that had taken a direct hit and needed a major overhaul. To watch them all gathered out on the sidewalk as though we were tied together with elastic bands and to hear the goodbyes and feel the sadness in the air was difficult to say the least. The van lurched forward and the bands were broken, maybe forever. My sleep that night was worse than terrible as my heart thumped and my mind was in overdrive, while I thought of this inexcusable crime England had committed. Through broken restless sleep and held back tears the dawn finally came. I felt as though a truck had hit me, but I knew what I had to do. We had breakfast and checked out of St. David Hotel on a very wet morning. Our destination was the city of Birmingham, my birthplace, and it was about a three-hour drive. The rain let up so we could enjoy the scenery of Wales one more time. We arrived at our hotel in the city around 1130 am. We settled into our room, which was quite nice and more modern than what we had left. It was decided to check the cemetery in the District of Yardley. All at once I was staring at a huge spooky looking cemetery and my thoughts suddenly took me back in time. This was scary. I got a chill and the hair on my arms bristled. I was face to face with the real thing that was stored in my deep memory. The huge wrought iron entrance gate and matching fence with the pointed tips reaching skyward still seemed frightening in my mind. I had left it magnificent and full of history no doubt, but my childhood memories were full of fear and I was glad to have company at this time.

My brother Joseph in Australia would be pleased as our memories matched perfectly. I am quite sure we passed the school I had attended, but it was summer and no way to check it out. I vaguely remember cutting my ear swinging between two desks and going to the hospital for a stitch or two. None of my memories would join and this was frustrating trying to put this jigsaw together. There was no help in sight and never had been. A feeling of great despair clouded my mind like London fog and I felt very sad.

Yardley is where I was born, and apparently my mother and father had spent their lifetimes here. Luck was with us this day as the pleasant staff bent over backward to help us. They checked their files and gave us direction to my father's common gravesite, where he was put to rest December 17, 1947. His family had gone forever, how would anyone cope? My mother was cremated years later and her ashes scattered near the common grave. I did not feel emotion but I tried to reason and think, yet this proved impossible. What ever happened between them that tore them apart after I had left the country, I will never know. Maybe that is better, I think, to leave them at rest as God intended. We were all scattered then and are scattered now. Maybe the winds and storms of time will blow us back gently together again, as I would give you another chance. Who am I to judge, War is hell!

While Sheryl and I pondered in our silence the CBC mobile phone rang, and to my amazement the call was for me. It was Nicola calling from the Health Committee Office in London. Nicola told me to go home to Canada and write a letter for an appointment. I told her in no uncertain terms that the English Government had paid my fair after all these years to meet with family that I had no idea existed, and that the Government Agencies were to assist in answering any questions for the Child Migrant. The lady got rude and obnoxious. I told her of the letter I had from the Clerk of the Health Committee who wrote me on behalf of M.P. David Hartley Hinchcliffe, Chairman of her Committee. I had copies of two letters I had written them a good year prior to my arrival. Again, they failed to answer. Somebody at that office was lying through his or her teeth as we had tried to make contact before we left Canada on this historic journey. The Canadian Broadcasting Corporation Television spoke to David Serrant, no courtesy, and no call back.

When we arrived in England we had talked to Jason, who referred us to phone Mellisa, said to be away on vacation, and so the rudeness went. I asked Nicola who put her up to this horrible call, as I believe the culprit did not have the courage to shoulder this historic dirty work and sick injustice. I told her of the House of Commons Session 1997-1998, titled Health Committee Third Report. The Welfare of former Child Migrants. The report states, all Governments should show flexibility and understanding to all Child Migrants where documentation is concerned. They wrote that no children were shipped to Canada after 1939, along with many more lies. The English were pedaling the world a load of political B.S. to protect the wrongs and horror that they created. Nicola was told I had copies of their phony reports (what did she mean by phony reports). Conversation was tense and futile, and I told the lady I would show up the next day and they could reject me to my face. The call was rudely terminated by the lady. We left the cemetery, and I felt a little shaken and hurt by the recent telephone event.

Somehow the driver found the house I was born in. I have to say it felt strange standing in front of this little brick house, trying to recollect some words or mind pictures from so long ago. I heard what I thought was adults arguing and the sound of aircraft overhead. Scenes of playing in rubble created from many bombs being dropped entered my mind. A man and woman came out of the house and invited us to take pictures and to come inside to see where I was born. It was quite eerie, but I truly felt I had lived here in the past. They had lived there for thirty years and had done considerable renovation but could say no more. Back outside an aircraft flew over low and the couple said they were in the flight path of the airport that had been there during the war. The dreams I had of aircraft drones had been real and can now be put to rest.

We thanked them ever so much and we were off again through another maze of old buildings, an English history, back to the hotel. We split from the camera people and we toured the City of Birmingham by foot for part of the afternoon. Later, my cousin Derek came and picked us up. He had driven down from Wales to his home just outside Birmingham. After a light lunch Derek took us for a lovely drive through Birmingham City suburbs. I was lost and strained to recognize something, but to no avail. Derek drove us to our Uncle Lester's residence, but he was not home. On checking with neighbors, we found he had been hospitalized two days prior and were told he was quite ill. It was decided not to see him as he was in his eighties and the shock might not do him well. Derek was in touch and would surely relay our sadness at not meeting him as he had so wished. Hopefully he could enjoy the Canadian salmon and Maple syrup we dropped off for him. We then drove to my cousin Nancy's home. Nancy could not visit in Wales due to prior commitments. Her husband Glenn showed up and we had a beautiful visit but again, too short. A sad goodbye and back to the hotel. We had supper with Derek and bid farewell again. I thought of my Canadian family, including my dog Nikita. I hit the bed with mixed emotions and slept from pure exhaustion.

Middlemore Homes, August 21

Morning came after a good sleep and we were ready to meet another day. After a light breakfast we were off to the Birmingham Library to look at records of my past, which made my heart beat a little faster at facing more of the unknown. CBC Television had made this possible. My, my, the power of the press is amazing. Some records were interesting and filled in a few blanks but nothing too exciting. Sadly, there were no pictures of me but I did see two of my brother Joseph who was shipped to Australia many years ago. Most records are incomplete, useless, and full of untruths. Then we were off to meet the General Secretary of Middlemore Emigration Homes where they shipped English babies around the world. Their mission was "to get rid of diseased tissue from English streets"[3].

---

3.   British House of Commons Hansard, May 1999

As we had been referred to, but history records state the aim was to send us to Canada and Australia Fairbridge farms to be trained for colonial farm life, and both Governments waived the under the age of 14 clause, where those under the age of 14 had to be accompanied by an adult. The secretary was very nice but not very helpful, as her knowledge appeared to be limited.

Middlemore Homes was a few miles away but Michael, our English driver, found the way and soon we pulled into a driveway that I recognized. The huge buildings called the Middlemore Homes that had been surrounded in rubble from the war brought back crystal-clear memories and I could hardly keep my thoughts in check. The buildings and grounds had hardly changed in all these years gone by. This is where I had spent some war years. The home was connected to deceit. Cadbury's Chocolate Company was rumored to be involved heavily in the trafficking of Middlemore children along with the Birmingham Board of Education. Many others who exploited young babies and children were never seen. Their dark secrets they hoped would be buried till the end of time. They did not count on the erosion of time and these babies growing up and coming back to haunt them. Some folk may have thought it was a good idea to split families up, but time proved how totally wrong they were.

The manager at Middlemore was very kind and let us take film and pictures and look everything over. I could not believe they were still involved with young people with problems. I entered the main building and, much to my surprise, the linoleum in the big main hall was green in color and very old looking. My brother Joseph had mentioned to check out the color when I was in Australia and we had agreed on the color green. I chose to believe it was the same flooring as when we were there. Sounds of war entered my mind and it felt good to re-live memories, but spooky as well.

I remembered certain rooms and the way to the bomb shelter. The field where Babs the horse lived was the same. I could see her clearly in my mind along with the old orchard where apples used to grow. More pictures rolled through my mind as though they had been stored there for future reference. The sight of small children picking dandelion leaves in the pasture and putting them in a grey metal tub to be washed.

I reached down and picked a dandelion leaf and held it till the wail of the 'all clear' siren left my head for maybe the last time. Tears formed in my eyes as there were no true answers for me, and I witnessed so many lies. It was hard to comprehend what fellow man could do to their own kind. While standing in Middlemore Homes, I was wanting to hate my mother, for I learned that she admitted each of us in this home, but did she of her own accord? I remember reading the many untruths and coverups, and also learning that some mothers were coerced into giving up their children, and that the Colonies needed colonial farm labour. Some thought their children were adopted out and did not know their children continued to live in orphanages and foster homes across the seas. How to know the real answers, in the end I have to choose to believe she did this for her own well-being and mine. Coerced or not.

Fairbridge-London, August 22

We had arrived in London and met with staff at the Fairbridge Office. I was presented with some records of my childhood that came from the Archives in the City of Liverpool. Gil the Fairbridge spokesperson suggested not to read these records alone. It was like a scene from a James Bond movie and I could hardly wait. I asked who found the records in all that dust of time, and we had a laugh. However, after reading records carefully with my wife Sheryl, ninety-five percent made no sense at all, who wrote this and why? Some were impossible to be true, such as having the lad rejoin his mother and father in Australia in the 1960s. Father was dead, and mother had never set foot on Australian soil. Plus, I was married to my wife Sheryl in 1963. No mention of Middlemore Homes or why I was immigrated to Canada. The reason, I feel, is that I was sent to a foreign land illegally and now the real battle begins. This tells why nobody who could get involved will; they are stifled by embarrassed bureaucracy.

We bid farewell to the pleasant staff and we decided to go underground and ride the tube. People and trains all over the place! All of a sudden, I wished I were back in Canada. Sheryl and I agreed it was too much for our lifestyle. Sheryl did not like the dark underground even though it was only an experience, she found it spooky. Soon we were looking at Big Ben, Westminster Abbey, and Parliament Square just a little way off. The history in England is mind boggling and the city of

London is breathtaking while loaded with history. I thought after this long journey it would have been so nice for one official to welcome this Child Migrant home to the country he was born in. This was not to be, and it left more than a bitter taste and a few choice words in my mouth. My mind wandered over the ocean to Canada and our way of life in the countryside. We gazed across and down the Thames River and watched the water traffic for some time. I tried to compare it to the mighty Fraser River back home but that is impossible. They are both unique in their own way, but I prefer the Mighty Fraser River.

Health Committee Visit

This was the final stop of this bureaucratic nightmare of charades and hide-and-go-seek in this little country. It was also the most important stop of the tour. This was where the lies of the Welfare of British Child Migrants were formulated to tell the rest of the world. The War was long over for some, but England continued to distort the truth over fifty-five years later. Little people like me that didn't have the power to blow our horn around the world, like England, had to pay the consequences. Our only chance, as in all evil, was to carry on the relentless struggle to let the world know the truth about England's dark side against their own babies and why they continue to lie, hide, and torment what used to be their own.

Owning the truth helps all to move on. On September 11, 2001 the United States of America took a cruel and vicious blow below the belt. This was something not common for our Canadian neighbours and close friends, and my heart went out to them. As I watched the tragedy unfold on the television screen, I was reminded once again of the lies and deceit of the British government. The Prime Minister of England was saying on American television that three hundred Britons were lost in the World Trade Center disaster, "The greatest loss since the Second World War", he claimed. I agree, but *Good God man, don't you know your history!? What about the disaster England created by exiling thousands of good British white stock babies? This happened after the War was over, why won't anyone talk about this?!* We were across the street from the Health Committee Offices deciding our plan of action. The street was fairly busy with traffic so as pedestrians, we blended right in. We knew that we were not welcome here from previous conversation. A man appeared on the sidewalk in front of the Health Committee Building. He looked up and down Waterloo Street and the surrounding area. Feeling satisfied, he entered the building but reappeared a minute or two later to check again. It was obvious he was some kind of security personnel. His actions and uniform told the tale.

My wife Sheryl, myself, and the producer of this documentary (who had a camcorder ready to film) entered the building. We did this a moment or two after the man re-entered after checking the street again. The man was startled, and I tried to explain who I was. This man went ballistic and began yelling at the female operating the camera. *"Turn it off and get out of here!"* he fumed. I asked him if the camera left, could I stay. *"I was told to expect you people and not to let you in here"*, he exclaimed. The man was rude and was losing control. I asked where the staff was, and he mumbled that they were all away for the day. He repeated the words, *"leave the building"*. I hoped that he would call the police, as I had suggested, but he did not. This disappointing and sad moment had happened, and nobody could change it. We exited the building with the man still expounding. Outside, the CBC TV crew had a camera and sound set up on the sidewalk. The security man started yelling at the cameraman, *"Get away from here, your film will be confiscated!"* The reply was *"Sir, we are on public property"*. The poor guy looked hopelessly defeated in his quest to do this nasty work for some very weak individuals.

I thanked my family and the ordinary British people that we had the great pleasure of meeting. The laughter and sadness we all shared will linger in my heart forever. This saga of finding and receiving records of my childhood was over. We were still left with incomplete records, years missing of my infant years. There seemed to be many untruths swapped back and forth between incompetent people of the time. I shall 'never say never' as this is far from over, but rather suspended in time again. The War however still rages on as the march for truth is on the horizon. Seeking the truth will be difficult, but a journey I must take to ease newfound pain that lingers in my heart at every beat and every breath I take.

January 25, 2002 - After Health Office Fiasco

My wife and I went for a good walk, looked through shops, and marveled at the history of this very old country. We stopped in a Quaint English Pub, ate bangers and mash, drank a fine English Lager beer, had terrific conversation, and answered many questions about Canada. We were joined by a friendly couple from Nova Scotia, which is on the East

Coast of Canada, and swapped stories and much laughter. My sadness was tucked away for a little while, but only a little while.

My sleep that night was broken, tossing and turning as pictures and thoughts overloaded my mind like debris in outer space. *"Was this trip a lesson in futility?"*, I pondered. *"Should things have been left alone, as I was for so many years?"* I fought off the faintness and strain that my mind and soul were under. I clambered back on my survival train and won the battle to stay on track. I looked at my wife and wondered after all these years of standing by her man, if I deserved her. I never realized my burden had become her silent one as she accepted me for who I am. A smile came on my face and I thought, *"Some things are indeed, meant to be"*. I promised to learn to show more emotion, and openness with love, if possible.

I tried to be quiet as I took a shower, and silently thanked God for his divine intervention and power. You see, He made sure I would not be alone. He worked His magic and gave me the opportunity to share my life with this special person, my wife. God is about love, not hate. It is the decision and choices people make that create hate and hardships. I am so grateful I was awake enough to recognize the love for my wife and her love to me. My singing woke Sheryl up, and we got ready to meet the day.

We said goodbye to the camera crew and Kathy, the producer of this documentary, over a fine English breakfast. We checked out of the Sydney Hotel, but not before making four local phone calls. The calls were expensive, just like the cost of staying in a hotel. Out on the street the noise of jackhammers, demolition, and construction greeted us. We went for another nice walk and absorbed more history in this foreign land.

Rod had come all the way from the City of Birmingham, a two-hour drive to pick us up for the drive back to the Midlands. The motorways continued to amaze me. There were many of them and many lanes to choose from, but so much traffic that at times they were at a complete standstill. I made a vow then not to grumble at our mostly wide-open spaces back at home. We arrived at Rod's home to be reacquainted with three of his daughters – Nicola, Samantha, and Lorna. Natasha would join us soon. As the English say, "I was completely knackered". After sharing many stories, we got to bed and slept the English night away.

Trip to Bristol Bay

Morning came quickly and it looked like a sunny day ahead. Rod had to drive to Bristol (about a two-hour drive) for business. I went along for the ride and was glad I did. When we arrived at the seaside at Bristol Bay, the tide was out and the beach was full of activity on this beautiful day. Rod parked the car and we walked down this very long pier to a building that was an arcade. We went inside. It was totally amazing. There were gambling machines, rides for children, and things to attract tourists and their own to this magical place on the seaside. I pondered, "There is nothing at home that I have seen that comes close to what I have enjoyed this day". After getting our fill of ice cream and chips, it was time to head back. The English countryside was beautiful. We got home, tired yet satisfied, but not before stopping at a quaint pub for a pint. My wife Sheryl and Lorna had spent a great day together and presented us with a supper fit for a King. Evening came quickly and I wondered where the day had gone.

After Bristol Bay

The next morning, we enjoyed a lovely English breakfast that Rod insisted on fixing with no help. We decided to simply relax for the day. This suited Sheryl and I just fine, as we could recharge our batteries. Evening came and we decided to go to a local pub. It was not karaoke, but people could get up and sing if they fancied. I thought that some folks were quite good, but maybe it was just the alcohol.

The next day we drove into the city of Birmingham and arrived at a huge marketplace. It reminded us of a flea market in Canada, but far more extensive. The vendors sold everything from meat, fish, poultry, seafood, to buttons and bows. You name it, they had it. I had a baked potato, English style, with lots of butter. It was excellent.

We toured another part of Birmingham and took in some more history, then arrived at the address, 125 Florence Street. This area looked vague to me but seemed a little familiar, as documents say my Mum had lived here at some time during the Second World War.

My distant memory told me that I had been there during a bombing. In the distant haze, my memory believed I played in the rubble of bombed out buildings. If it was quiet, my mind could let me listen to the sounds of aircraft, sirens, whistling bombs, and such. I could hear the sound of other children and the chatter as we played in the rubble of war. Could these other children have belonged to me? My guess is, only God could answer that!

Later that day we went to the cemetery where Pat (my sister) rested. I knelt and said a silent prayer to her and was thankful. I believed that she would be thankful that her family had been found at last. Pat's sorrow and pain was over, and she could now rest in peace. I would forage on for the truth and understanding.

Caravan Park

Another day arrived, the last before we left for home. We drove to Kensington Price, a quaint village where the pottery factories are located. Beautiful Chinaware was made and shipped around the world from this reclusive little place. Rod and I spent some time watching a potato jacket machine that turned out those delicious baked potatoes that were increasing my weight. We spent the evening packing suitcases. The longing for home was growing strong, and I realized that travel was not meant for me. Before first light, I was up and had the car loaded.

We were on our way early to Heathrow after saying somber goodbyes to the girls. Heathrow airport was about a two- and one-half hour drive. We arrived safely, thanked, and said goodbye to Rod. It was 1:50 PM and we were sitting on a loaded 747 aircraft. It was warm – super warm – and we did not get the seats we were promised months ago. I was over the darn wing that I definitely had no desire for. The Captain reported there was a problem securing one of the cargo doors and we had missed our place in line for take-off, which created another twenty-minute delay. Finally, fresh air was circulated, and people settled down. The flight attendant started the safety film and soon apologized for the breakdown of the safety video. Finally, we got off the ground one hour and twenty minutes late. This was understandable for safety reasons, but the service during the flight was awful, and there was a great deal of grumbling from many passengers. It seemed like an eternity as we sat in this aluminum can, but I was able to finally relax with only thoughts of home and my family in my head – and, of course, my dog Nikita.

Touchdown was smooth, we cleared the airport and were homeward bound. I had one final thought for those few rude British people in London, *"With help and strength, the world will know the truth".*

September 20, 2002 – Brother Joe Visit to Canada

Sheryl and I arrived at the Vancouver Airport early, as we lived in the City of Abbotsford which was a good hour's drive through heavy traffic. At the terminal we checked the time of incoming flights. My brother Joe and his wife Diana were on the Airline Cathay Pacific from Hong Kong, which would land at 11:29 A.M. We had about a half hour to people watch, observe the different attire (some extremely colorful), and hear many different languages. I would never get used to such hustle and bustle but indeed it was interesting. My wife Sheryl on the other hand, has the patience of a Saint and thoroughly enjoyed looking in all the shops at souvenirs offered to travelers from around the world.

We checked the arrivals and realized the aircraft had landed. My excitement was mounting. The thought entered my mind that fourteen hours ago they had been in Hong Kong. The world was definitely smaller in this age of technology. Sheryl picked Joe and Diane out on a television monitor and they were heading our way. Within minutes we were together again. The feeling behind my eyes was one of tremendous pressure but I held back again, a cloud filled with tears.

We headed for our car, happy as meadowlarks with everyone wanting to talk at once. Joe immediately went for the driver's side of the car as I watched with much glee! In Australia where they live "down under" their steering wheel is the opposite side to North American vehicles. Joe finally got used to this about two days before they had to leave but believe me, it was amusing to watch his expression each time he approached a vehicle on the wrong side. There was much chatter on the way home, and I immediately took on the role of tour guide, to answer the many questions and explain just what they were looking at.

On the Road from the Airport

I could thank my past and all the places I had lived and worked, as my knowledge of the city of Vancouver and the entire province of Beautiful British Columbia was a picture-perfect road map in my mind. I felt an incredible warmth come over me and found myself looking in the mirror of life and comparing the similarities of two brothers that had been separated, for what could have been till eternity. I was three years older, so the records say. I spoke Canadian, and Joe spoke Australian. Our sense of humor and laughter were very similar, as were the construction of our bodies. I am more hyper; at least that's what they would have me believe. Neither Joe nor Diane seemed to have suffered Jet Lag, as when we arrived at our home, we all seemed to have an awful thirst. Our connection was amazing and after getting them settled and freshened up we settled into sharing the adventures of our lives. We discussed marriage, children, grandchildren and yes, even a greatgrandchild as we tried to unite our family from afar.

I told Joe about our English Family that I had met in August 2001. A family he had never heard of or met; we had a lot to catch up on, but we would need another lifetime to accomplish this goal. Deep inside me, on the shelf in my dusty memory of time was a book entitled "*Hatred of the British Empire*". This book was never written, but all the words are forever present, sitting there, waiting for the command to put this tragedy in print. I sometimes pray that some miracle will help me improve my skills to get this story out, as it is a part of shameful history.

September 30, 2002 - Meeting My Perfect Canadian Family

We decided to leave Abbotsford for a few days and show our guests the interior of the province of British Columbia. Our brother-in-law Ted (affectionately known as Teddy Bear), and his wife Myrtle (Sheryl's sister, whom I called Turtle) had retired to the town of Osoyoos in the southeast part of British Columbia some years back. This was our destination. Sheryl's other sister Margaret and husband Donald would travel at the same time. We would meet with them at a quaint mountain town called Princeton, nestled near the east end of the Cascade Mountain Range. We would meet at our favorite place for a truly Canadian breakfast. Joe and Diane were absolutely thrilled with the scenery as we headed up, around, down, and over the summit of the Allison Pass.

The beautiful, untouched snow-capped mountains were like a picturesque painting and the cool clear water of rivers and streams created a frame that took their breath away. They sighed as they observed twenty Mountain Sheep grazing near the roadside. I was hoping they might have seen other wildlife such as deer, moose, bear, or mountain goats. However, they had plenty to absorb already and we were just starting this adventure. With breakfast over and sixty-five miles to go, the change in scenery was very noticeable. We drove along beside the clear and smooth flowing Similkameen River, and past several campsites. Local residents and tourists both enjoying the beauty of the great outdoors would stop to rest or take pictures of this total magnificence that nature presented. We approached Osoyoos and stopped at a view site high on a hill. Osoyoos Lake was below. The arid dryness of the desert was dotted with orchards and vineyards wherever there was irrigation. It was a picture on many postcards. The town of Osoyoos had a resident population of approximately five thousand. Being a tourist town for at least four months of a given year meant it could swell to standing room only, meaning no vacancy. Some of the locals detested the summer invasion of tourists and city folk. They forgot what it did for their economy. Quite often, this little town was the hot spot in Canada and had the added attraction of a beautiful lake to swim in and enjoy water sports.

We arrived at Murt and Ted's, and introductions were made. Their home was big, beautiful, and air conditioned, as the temperature was in the 26-degree Celsius range and climbing. It did not bother the Australians, but I had to seek cover now and then. Once settled in, my Canadian family became easily acquainted with my family from the other side of the world. In no time it was as if they had been around us a long time and we had a wonderful stay with Murt and Ted. One day we took them further North in the Okanagan, through small towns with names like Oliver, O.K. Falls, and Kaleden on our way to the city of Penticton.

It was a shame that they could not see the Okanagan Valley during blossom time, but that was back in April and May. However, fresh fruit was always plentiful such as peaches, apples, apricots, prunes, pears, cantaloupe, grapes, and much more. We stopped and tried our luck in a casino and Joe managed to win one hundred and twenty-five dollars. The rest of us were not that lucky – maybe next time. I pointed out to them that thousands of lakes dot this great province. In particular, Okanagan Lake, which was home to the world-famous Ogopogo, and Skaha Lake, another lake of beauty with its sandy beaches. I don't believe they had seen this much fresh water in their life, a commodity we take for granted. Joe told us that the dam holding the water supply for the city of Perth Australia where he lives is at seventeen percent capacity. He was amazed at people sprinkling their lawns even though I told him we have water restrictions, but he could not understand why.

September 30, 2002

Diane and Joe treated us to Chinese food, and we headed south to Ted's for more fun and endless laughter. 'Donald' volunteered Joe and I's services to Teddy Bear. Teddy was building a dock like the kind you tie a boat to. He needed forty 2x6 boards coated with a preservative. It was the first time in my life I had worked with my brother. He had picked up similar skills as I did in the crappy orphanage called Fairbridge, but his was in a place called Pinjarra, in the outback of Australia. We got the painting done in record time as Donald Duck and Teddy Bear were still pounding nails into the wooden part of the dock. I forgot to mention that most of us have nicknames. Donald and Margaret are known as Donald and Daisy Duck.

October 1, 2002 – Leaving Osoyoos

As I lay awake in bed, I can hear the stillness of the night. My eyes wide open and my mind, projecting picture as to what might have been. Sadness is part of everybody's well-being. But maybe more so for people caught up in the strange happenings that the cards of life have dealt their loved ones. History hidden from the outside world so as not to embarrass a nation by bringing their war crimes to the surface. To float the horrendous truth in front of a civilized world. Six decades have gone by for me and I have had the love of my wife and her family for over forty years. No, my grown-up life had not all been sad, but the damage to my childhood was beyond repair. I felt a dampness in my eyes and held back the urge to cry, as some greater force held my feelings back. I eventually drifted off to a mixed and broken sleep and before I knew it, the dawn was breaking.

Donald was up and had the coffee on and I got washed and joined him. I never discuss too much of my inner clouds of sadness that appear much too often. I am a man now and try to conceal feelings that are strong enough to break hearts. The rest of the gang was up now, and we packed the cars and said our good-byes. I was happy that the family had accepted the Australian family with so much feeling and heart. We are on the road again, talking about the pleasant things we had done, and the memories created forever. Being together as a family was the intention of God, and it took evil people to defy those wishes.

Harrison Hot Springs

After a day of rest and laughter, Sheryl suggested we drive to a place called Harrison Hot Springs. As luck would have it, there was a world class sandcastle competition going on. People from around the world flying flags from many nations, pitted their talents against one another in the quest for first prize. There is no way I could have been a judge, as I thought that all of the entries were remarkable. With the mountains as a backdrop to Harrison Lake, the quaint resort village had its own special identity. We stopped at a sidewalk cafe to quench our thirst and to swallow the beauty of a perfect day. We passed a very old barn in immaculate condition and Diana just had to have a picture. I obliged and I pulled the car into the farmyard. Luck was with us, as the farmer was near the barn splitting wood. He gave permission, so Diana and Sheryl took pictures of this eighty-year-old barn as Joe tried to converse with the farmer. Back in the car, Joe reported to me that the farmer had told him there were barn owls that were so big they had to fly through the huge barn door sideways. Working on many farms in my youth I knew the old farmer was pulling Joe's leg. I had to go with the thought till I burst out laughing, sputtering the sound "*Hoot, hoot*".

I wished these days spent together would never end, but the clock was ticking. I think we all felt we would like the power to stop the clock, or at least turn it back. But as we know, time waits for no one. We went home and planned for the next adventure.

Stave Lake Power Dam

We were driving north, across the Mission Bridge that spans the mighty Fraser River that captivates the mind, and its beauty can take your breath away. Unfortunately, today is a little off weather wise and looks like rain. Our journey took us into the district of Mission, a small but thriving community built between the Fraser River and the mountains to the north. I started gaining altitude, as the area was quite hilly and relied on my memory to guide our way. I had not been up in these hills for about twenty years but not much had changed other than the growth of the trees.

We arrived at the Stave Lake Dam and followed signs down below the dam to the powerhouse where the turbines created electricity. If we had been a day early, we could have toured the power plant but there was still plenty to see. We could see the spillway designed for excess water and it brought back a memory from my past. I had picnicked just down river from where we were, over fifty years ago. We would go by boat above the man-made channel into the real Stave Lake to fish for Dolly Varden Trout. Back then, the channel (although marked for safety), was full of protruding "dead heads" (old tree stumps and trunks above and below the water line which could be dangerous to the inexperienced boater).

I drove up, crossed over the Dam, and found a place to park as there was no stopping on the Dam itself. Diana wanted pictures even though the weather was looking mean. I said we must hurry as I suspected the skies were about to open and we would get drenched in a hurry. We were now on top of the Dam, cameras clicking at this forlorn mass of mist, cloud, and dampness. A clap of thunder rolled straight over head and I hollered to run for the car. We just managed to pile in the car and another roll of thunder followed by lightening ripping out of the almost dark sky. That last clap of thunder and lightning snapped Diana's head to attention. I casually told her it was normal for this part of the world. Now they knew why everything was so green, as they envied our trees and forests. Windshield wipers on full, along with the windshield defrosters going full bore. Some vehicles had pulled over till this mini storm subsided. I could see the end of the storm where it met blue sky and it was behind us just that quick. I decided we would take a small Ferryboat back across the Fraser River to a little town called Fort

Langley. The Ferry held about thirty vehicles and we had to wait for two sailing's, which was about thirty minutes. It gave us the opportunity to eat some home-made french fries we bought nearby and have a close up look at the river.

On the south side of the river, we visited the Historic Fort Langley. It was our lucky day as staff were dressed in period costume of an era gone by and were anxious to answer all questions from the Aussie tourists. It was a trading post for the Hudson Bay Company to sell wares to trappers, miners, natives, and gold seekers. The Fraser River was the choice of transportation and hence, made the Fort very busy. Joe showed a keen interest in the furs of different animals still native to this great land. We toured all the buildings and read about the Fort's history. I took them to the Fort Hotel, which has the look of architecture long gone by, but quite modern. It was a nice place to have a drink and talk about our day.

After a good night's sleep and another hearty breakfast prepared by Sheryl, I decided to call Joe and I the 'flubber' brothers. We were putting on a few pounds and it was noticeable. We convinced each other that it was a holiday, and we would sweat it off later. The salmon fishing season was underway, and Sheryl took them for a drive to find and buy some fresh Sockeye. I took this time to mow the lawn and do a few chores. They arrived back about four hours later laughing, with three beautiful Sockeye, fresh and cleaned. Sheryl would make the brine and I would show Joe how the fish was prepared before placing it in my homemade stainless-steel smoker that I had in the yard. The fish was cut up into manageable pieces and placed in the brine for about twelve hours. Taken out of brine and patted down, ready to put in the smoker. I had the wood chips already mixed, cherry, apple, hickory, and some alder that worked well for us. I loaded the fish on three refrigerator size racks that handled three, seven or eight-pound Sockeye quite easily.

The chips were placed in a cast iron frying pan which sat on a hot plate below the racks. We were ready and I plugged the hot plate into power. This was going well, and it would not be long before the air was filled with that magical aroma of salmon being smoked. Expected time of cure was three to four hours in the homemade smoker. As in the past, the fish turned out perfect and I watched in glee as Joe and Diana gobbled it up like there was no tomorrow. They claimed they had never tasted anything like it, and I was pleased to accommodate them. While we were eating salmon and enjoying a beer, wine in Diana's case, I told them that while they were gone for the fish I had made some phone calls and lined up an excellent day trip. I did not tell details, except it involved a train and they would have to get up a tad earlier. They were gung-ho for what turned into a nice surprise.

The Train and the Harbor

We were up early, as we had to drive to District of Mission to catch the train to the city of Vancouver. This service was called the West Coast Express and was an alternate way for commuters to leave their vehicles and enjoy a stress-free ride on public transit to their place of work. We were to catch the 7:27am but we arrived a bit earlier than planned. With help getting our tickets from very pleasant staff we got on the 7:00am with twenty seconds left to departure. As the train moved silently forward, it occurred to me that we were all sharing this experience for the first time. From where we were seated in the second level, we would have the best view. There was a light mist, but that was to disappear shortly as a beautiful day was to be ours. The train was so smooth, without that rickety-rack sound I remembered from my past rail-roading experience. The train made its way parallel to the Fraser River for some time and there was much to see as the mist had lifted. Small sawmills and industry along the shoreline, log-booms and barges being towed by tugboats. Fishermen on the banks trying for an early catch of elusive salmon. I was very familiar with the entire route, as I had lived on this side of the river for a while as a boy working on farms and attending school. We passed the Albion Ferry that we had been on and continued on to veer a little North, away from the river.

We left behind outlying cities and towns as we got closer to Vancouver. The sun was waking up and all of a sudden, the Pacific Ocean was in view. This area was called the Burrard Inlet and the waters were calm and pristine. The only ripples on the water at this time were from small craft out fishing. I remembered watching high speed power boats reaching speeds of one hundred and forty miles per hour. This event drew huge crowds and took place in the early nineteen fifties. Vancouver Burrard Inlet was opening the way to the Second Narrows that was spanned by the Ironworkers Memorial Bridge. This connected Vancouver to North Vancouver. Twenty-eight men had died when the bridge had collapsed while under construction in 1958. I remembered this well, as I was on the old bridge a day or two later. I was home on leave from the airbase on the East Coast showing the beauty of BC to young air force friends. It was indeed a tragedy to be remembered and sadness for many.

The train was stopping at the end of the line, but not before showing a spectacular view of the Vancouver Harbor known as the gateway to the Pacific Rim. The ride from Mission had taken about one hour and twenty minutes. All this for eighteen dollars, that included all connecting transits for the entire day. We soon found a food fair where we had a light breakfast and then we were off again. We were now in the hustle and bustle of a major city. Very tall buildings blocked out the sun. We walked the couple of city blocks back toward the station as we could catch a bus to the world-famous Stanley Park, one thousand acres of forested magnificence and beauty that stole one's heart. By asking questions we boarded the correct bus number 135, which went directly to the park.

After a fifteen-minute ride we are walking to what was called the Seawall. It was built to protect the Park perimeter from the sea as storms could and have started erosion. The Seawall path is about ten kilometers and goes completely around the park. Young use it and old fit people, and not so fit. People on rollerblades, bicycles, walkers, and joggers. I have not seen a place in the world that is equal. We chose to walk as we could stop together and discuss the sights and take pictures. We are approaching the Lions Gate Suspension Bridge that spans the first narrows.

Lions Gate Bridge

The Lions Gate Bridge was constructed about 1938. It is a suspension bridge that crosses the first narrows waterway and connects Vancouver to West Vancouver. Some of Canada's wealthiest people live in luxurious homes with million-dollar views. A lot of these dwellings are built high up on the mountainsides where wild animals used to roam at leisure. From this height they have unobstructed views of Freighters swaying gently at anchor, waiting to get to port to load or unload their wares from around the world, to seeing the huge cruise ships leaving the harbor for a cruise to Alaska. The tide has to be just right in order to pass under the Lion's Gate Bridge. The float plane engines roaring to gain altitude to clear the bridge and the majestic mountains that loom in the background with their snow-capped peaks. I told them that when I was very young, my first family paid a twenty-five-cent toll to cross this bridge. That was about 1950 and the so-called British Properties were under development, hence the face of mountains started to change as man was on the move.

The bridge had just received a face-lift for the tune of seventy-six million dollars. They claimed it was an engineering marvel and I would have to agree. A brand-new deck was installed in prefabricated sections and some of the work was shown on television. Other than an inconvenience to some, it was widely acclaimed. We headed along a trail back into the tranquility of Stanley Park. We met a couple who told us about a free tour bus that came by every fifteen minutes. Sure enough, along came this wooden looking bus contraption and on we got. The driver's name was Bob; he wore a microphone and informed all passengers of different points of interest.

Bob the Bus Driver

Before you know it, the bus is full of mostly tourists from Hong Kong and Asia. I had trouble picking out the English language. Bob kept me in stitches because I think on this run, he was talking to himself. He was the man for the job and then he boldly announced that he was one of only fifteen percent in the area that was a true born Canadian. Still, no one seemed to be listening and he babbled on. That excellent tour over, we doubled Bob's gratuity and bid him farewell. The bus arrived to take us back to the station and we were pleased with our journey through the Park. There was a huge cruise ship called the Infinity. She was docked at Canada Place. A gorgeous facility designed to accommodate tourists from around the world. We could see people on the upper decks that looked the size of ants.

Joe and Diane wanted to ride on our Rapid Transit for it was nearby and ran every few minutes. I told them the little trains were without drivers and ran by computer on electric rails. We agreed on a run that would take us through three cities and high across the mighty Fraser River on yet another bridge. The end of the line was at King George station in the city of Surrey. We would ride round trip nonstop and Joe sat where a driver might have been. It was a good way to sightsee, as the passenger cars were modern and air-conditioned. The windows were big and offered far more to see compared to the car. Joe said he felt he was riding a roller coaster and was extremely pleased with his adventure. We got back to the station and now we had to get something to eat. We decided to take the Sea Bus, a people only boat that plied the harbor from Vancouver to the North Shore where we had heard of delicious seafood. Our voyage would take about fifteen minutes.

Quay in North Vancouver

The Sea Bus docked in North Vancouver and it is a short walk to the Lonsdale Quay. The smell of food near the fresh sea air was overwhelming and our search for Oysters began. It did not take long to find the place my niece Tracy had told me about. The others had become undecided now as there was so much to choose from. I did not hesitate and ordered Oysters with French Fries, and glad I did as they were delicious. Everyone was happy with their choice. We topped that off with a soft ice cream cone and got a burst of new energy. After a good look around the Quay we were back on the Sea Bus, heading back across the harbor to the station.

Our time had gone quickly, and we boarded the train in for Mission with ten minutes to spare. We got good seats in the Dome Car on the opposite side to pick up what we missed on the way in. As the train wound its way out of the city we reminisced about the day and the fun we had. The river was calm and threaded its way like a ribbon, parallel to the unending tracks of steel. Joe excitedly pointed to a spot in the river where a salmon had jumped and we could make out the circle of water disturbance. On closer observation the salmon jumped again, but this time I spotted a fisherman on the far bank. He had this fish hooked and was having the time of his life trying to land it. We don't know for sure, but we believe the fisherman won that battle. For the next little while things were quiet as we reflected our own thoughts as the train pulled into Mission Station. We found the car and headed for home, a little tired after twelve hours of nonstop play and adventure.

Goodbye and Farewell

My heart was busy reminding me of the positives and good things in my life, to help soften the inevitable of saying goodbye. But the scale always balanced with equal sadness, as I knew this could be the last time together. We spent the last day or two closer to home. Fish and chips at the resort town of White Rock with the Pacific Ocean and sandy beaches, we watched the tide. Tomorrow we would say goodbye. They had seen so much and met so many, yet so much more was left to do; sadly, there was no time.

I was extremely pleased they had met my first Mum this day, as she is almost ninety-five and had been eager to meet Joe and Diana. At her age, her accomplishments baffle one's mind as she learned the computer at age eighty-nine. Visually impaired, three books have been published about her life and worldly travels. This feat was done from memory of the past and a great motivation for all people to enjoy a full life. Mrs. Harris (previously known as Mrs. Lovick), my first Mum has inspired me in my quest to place pen in hand and tell my story. Not only did we have a fine lunch, her treat, but she also signed all three books as a gift to Joe and Diana. I always had trouble with the word love, but I have to say, I loved my first Mum.

Leaving on a Jet Plane

As we left for the airport, we still had laughter, but our faces did not show the same joy. The tune went through my mind, "I'm leaving on a Jet Plane, never to come back again". Over and over it played, and my heart filled with sadness that no human should endure. I held back emotions I had never had to use much on my path of life. At the airport we spent our last hour together discussing what we may do in the future. No promises, nothing written in stone, but the lifeline of love will never be broken. It was time to leave for the departure area, a trip they would take without us. Our goodbyes and hugs were quick, and I felt a transfer of love leave my body.

I thank God for my wife Sheryl, family, and our many friends for showing them kindness, love, and acceptance in a world so far from theirs.

Like the Olympic Flame, one day the Child Migrant Torch will light up the world. What crime did I, or my brother and sisters commit that tore us apart forever? Should children be punished and separated because of what adults did during a war we did not start? I hoped the other children in my group had a reasonable life.

Years later, contact with some tells me different, as they too were put on a different path leading to the long, cold road of lost love. How does a child forget or forgive a country that was supposed to love them? Maybe when worlds collide?

The cover is closed for now on this story that will never end.

PRESENT TIME

In 2021 I have reached the milestone of age 83 and with winter weather approaching I find myself warm and cozy in front of the fireplace, reflecting on the previous years. I started writing my story about 20 years ago. The pages sat collecting nothing but dust until with the help of friends, I paid it another visit. Living this horrendous history was not an easy thing, nor was re-living it throughout the pages of this book; however, it was time for light to be shone on the darkness that is my past, our past, a past that the Canadian government has so desperately tried to ignore. I am here to say that history can never stay hidden forever, and that it is time for Canada to speak up and share the truth of their part in this destruction that was so cruelly done to us children.

Britain and Australia have acknowledged their wrongdoing, a movie has been made, and CBC helped to get some answers; however, in 2021, Canada has yet to formally apologize for their actions that resulted in mine, and many other's torn childhoods. To this day, none of the immigration records from after 1935 have gone public. Immigrants themselves have a right to these files but they are kept hidden from the public. Through getting in touch with the British Columbia Archives in Victoria, I was provided little information but was informed that information regarding Fairbridge Farm School was placed in a time capsule and not to be opened until the year 2035. Closed to the public; however, that is not a time capsule. Why are these documents being hidden, what is it they are trying to hide? Is it because all of us war babies will be long gone by then and they hope to slip their wrong doings under the rug?

This story shares the raw truth, and it is the truth that has allowed me, at age 83, soon to be 84, to find a piece of freedom, and I hope it can do the same for the other forgotten children of war. Our story may have been ignored; however, it will now, never be forgotten. My name is Tom Isherwood, and this is my story-the best I could tell.

Written By: Thomas Isherwood

FAIRBRIDGE HISTORY

The below information has been derived from Wikipedia and Library and Archives Canada:

In 1909, South African-born Kingsley Fairbridge founded the *"Society for the Furtherance of Child Emigration to the Colonies"* which was later incorporated as the Child Emigration Society. The purpose of the society, which later became the Fairbridge Foundation, was to educate orphaned and neglected children and train them in farming practices at farm schools located throughout the British Empire. Fairbridge emigrated to Australia in 1912, where his ideas received support and encouragement.[7] According to the British House of Commons Child Migrant's Trust Report, "it is estimated that some 150,000 children were dispatched over a period of 350 years—the earliest recorded child migrants left Britain for the Virginia Colony in 1618, and the process did not finally end until the late 1960s."[8] It was widely believed by contemporaries that all of these children were orphans, but it is now known that most had living parents, some of whom had no idea of the fate of their children after they were left in care homes, and some led to believe that their children had been adopted somewhere in Britain.[9]

Child emigration was largely suspended for economic reasons during the Great Depression of the 1930s but was not completely terminated until the 1970s.[9,10] As they were compulsorily shipped out of Britain, many of the children were deceived into believing their parents were dead, and that a more abundant life awaited them.[11] Some were exploited as cheap agricultural labour, or denied proper shelter and education.[10,12] It was common for Home Children to run away, sometimes finding a caring family or better working conditions.[12]

---

7. Anon (22 November 2003). "English Orphan Transports: Fairbridge Foundation". *Historical Boys Clothing.* Retrieved 24 April 2010.

8. "Home Children," Wikipedia (Wikimedia Foundation, March 29, 2021), https://en.wikipedia.org/wiki/Home_Children.

9. "Ordeal of Australia's child migrants". *BBC News.* 15 November 2009. Retrieved 15 November 2009.

10. *"Cornish children sent abroad after migration stop: Unwanted children were sent to Australia by Cornwall County Council years after the practice had been discredited, BBC Cornwall has learned". BBC News. 1 February 2010. Retrieved 7 February 2019.*

11. "UK child migrants apology planned". *BBC News.* 15 November 2009. Retrieved 15 November 2009.

12. Stewart, Patrick. "The Home Children" (PDF). *pier21.ca.* Canadian Museum of Immigration at Pier 21. Archived from the original (PDF) on 20 April 2017. Retrieved 24 January 2017.

In 2014–2015 the Northern Ireland Historical Institutional Abuse Inquiry considered cases of children forcibly sent to Australia. They found that about 130 young children in the care of voluntary or state institutions were sent to Australia in what was described as the Child Migrant Programme in the period covered by the Inquiry, from 1922 to 1995, but mostly shortly after the Second World War. Children from the Middlemore Emigration Homes in England who came to Canada between 1936 and 1948 were brought here by the Fairbridge Society to their farm school in British Columbia.[13]

In 1913, the society started sending boys to a farm school in Australia. The Prince of Wales Fairbridge Farm School was opened in 1935 in Cowichan Station, located on Vancouver Island, near Duncan, British Columbia. It was named after one of their major supporters, the Prince of Wales (later King Edward VIII).[14]

The society had the support of the provincial and federal governments. A regulation that prohibited the immigration of unaccompanied children under the age of fourteen was waived. Students at the farm school lived in group cottages and were to receive a standard Canadian education up to the age of fifteen, then three years of vocational training. In 1938, Captain James Cameron Dun-Waters donated "Fintry", his orchard and dairy farm in the Okanagan Valley near Vernon, to the Fairbridge Society. Some of the older children from the Vancouver Island school worked at the Fintry Fairbridge Training Farm during the summers. Fairbridge also brought children from other agencies, including the younger Middlemore children. Also, Fairbridge children were first sent to the Middlemore Homes for training before emigration. Most were sent to Australia and smaller numbers to Canada. Emigration slowed during the Second World War and the Prince of Wales Fairbridge Farm School closed in 1949.[14]

---

13. Library and Archives Canada, "Home Children, 1869-1932," Library and Archives Canada, March 4, 2021, https://www.bac-lac.gc.ca/eng/discover/immigration/immigration-records/home-children-1869-1930/Pages/home-children.aspx.

14. Library and Archives Canada, "Fairbridge Society," Library and Archives Canada, May 4, 2018, https://www.bac-lac.gc.ca/eng/discover/immigration/immigration-records/home-children-1869-1930/home-children-guide/Pages/fairbridge-society.aspx

ACQUIRED SIXTY YEARS TOO LATE
BETTER LATE THAN NEVER THEY SAY

Email received from: Tony Wright MP, 2001:

Dear Mr. Isherwood

I understand that you have been e-mailing me. I regret that my office thought your e-mails were a circular to all MPs (of which we get too many to answer). Hence my failure to reply or even acknowledge. I apologize for this. The experience you describe was certainly an outrage. I have a constituent who was a victim of it. We have pressed the Government to do something to help the families involved, but this can never even begin to put right the great wrong that was done to them. I apologize again for not saying this to you more promptly.

Email received from Pierre 21- 2000:

From: library@pier21 in Nova Scotia
Tuesday, October 31, 2000
Subject: Pier 21

Dear Mr. Isherwood:

I have looked for the records of you and your siblings in the Home Children sources that I have without any luck. As I mentioned in my note yesterday David and Kay Lorente are the leading researchers in this area and may be able to help you. The Lorentes hosted a Home Children reunion here in August and spoke about the assistance program initiated by the British government to help reunite siblings and extended family separated by the movement. I distinctly remember them mentioning that the applications for funding made it almost impossible to prove that you were a Home Child so I fully understand your frustration. David and Kay can be contacted electronically.

I deeply regret that I cannot be of more assistance but my arrival schedules are incomplete and I do not have a record of the Aquitania calling in May of 1947. Many displaced persons were arriving during that era and most of those arrivals were unscheduled so that may explain it.

I just checked another source which lists arrivals that were confirmed through newspaper clippings and it seems that your ship called twice that month. It notes that the Aquitania arrived on May 3, 1947 carrying 1,492 passengers. Among them were war brides and 50 displaced people destined to families in Canada. The second arrival was on May 25th, 1947 with 500 workers on their way to farms in Canada. It says that they were veterans but you may have been among them.

We are just now starting a project to copy all of these articles but it will be slow. Here are the details in case you would like to contact our local library and order them yourself. Halifax Chronicle p.14, May 3, 1947 and Halifax Chronicle, May 20, 1947. The second has no page reference. Here is the address of the library which holds microfilm copies of these newspapers. Halifax Regional Library, 5381 Spring Garden Road, Halifax, Nova Scotia, B3J 1E9.

I hope that this little bit of information helps and that the Lorentes are able to direct your research. Please write back and let me know if you would be willing to allow us to add your story to our collection of immigration stories. Yours is the latest arrival of this kind that I have come across, indeed I did not even realize that Middelmore was still operating through the war years. Please consider sharing your experience with us but know that I fully understand if it is too personal.

Thank you for your letter and please let me know if there is any other way that I may be able to help.

The Best I Remember – A Cruel British Tragedy

SAVOY HOUSE, 115 STRAND, LONDON, W.C.2

Name of Child		Date of Birth
ISHERWOOD, Thomas John		12.38

(Birth certificate to be attached if available)

Present Address **Middlemore Emigration Homes, Weoley Park Road, Selly Oak,**
Address of Institution, if any, and reason for admission **do.** (For reason, see child's B'ham, 29.
Shenley Fields Cottage Homes, B'ham (P.A.) history overleaf).
School Standard **Jervoise Infants** Ability **average.**
Class I. (C. of E.)
Birthplace 14 Burnstocke Rd. Denomination *(School report to be attached)*
Lea Hall, Yardley, B'ham. Where Confirmed
Where Baptised St. Margaret's
By whom recommended West End, B'ham.

Committee of the Middlemore Emigration Homes

MOTHER	Name and Address **Elsie Isherwood, 1/25 Florence Street, Holloway Head,** B'ham, 1.	
	Occupation and Character **Housewife**	
	If dead, date and cause of death	
FATHER	Name and Address **William Isherwood, 45 Palmer Street, Off Garrison Lane** B'ham, 9.	
	Occupation and Character **Labourer**	
	If dead, date and cause of death	

BROTHERS AND SISTERS	Name	Age	Address and Employment
	Beryl Hazel	12	Fairbridge Hostel, Benington.
	Jeanette	8	Middlemore Homes
	Margaret Ellen	9	do.
	Joseph Harold	3	Middlemore Babies' Home

Nearest responsible relatives **Committee of the Middlemore Emigration Homes**
Any relations in the Dominions overseas? **No**
Is the child in receipt of an allowance under the Widows' and Orphans' Pension Act? **No**

REMARKS

Character and disposition of child **Normal.**
Is it necessary or has it been necessary for the Child to wear glasses? **No** Does the Child wet the bed? **No**
What illnesses has the Child had (including infectious complaints)? **Measles. Mumps. Ch.Pox. Whooping Cough.**
Has the Child been immunised against Diphtheria? **Yes** Height **3' 10"** Weight **3 st. 12 lbs.**
Vaccinated **Yes**
Signature of Person answering above *[signature]*

FAMILY HISTORY: PLEASE COMPLETE AND SIGN OVERLEAF

I/we hereby hand over the Child **Thomas John Isherwood**
to the FAIRBRIDGE FARM SCHOOLS SOCIETY for emigration to Canada or Australia and I promise to use no influence with a
view to removing **him** having of my/our free will placed **him** in the Society's charge and indemnify the Society
against any claims and demands that may arise in consequence of the Child being subsequently returned to this country. I also
authorise the Society to have such medical and surgical treatment carried out as may be necessary for my child's welfare

Signature of Parents or Guardian *[signature]*

Address **Middlemore Emigration Homes, Selly Oak, B'ham, 29.**

The Best I Remember – A Cruel British Tragedy

Government of   Gouvernement du
Canada   Canada
        CITIZENSHIP REGISTRATION   ENREGISTREMENT ET PROMOTION
         AND PROMOTION   DE LA CITOYENNETÉ

	Date		
	Y-A	M	D-J
	1992	08	12

THOMAS ISHERWOOD
2021 OAKRIDGE CRES.
CLEARBROOK, BRITISH COLUMBIA
V2S 4N5

COURT OF CANADIAN CITIZENSHIP
#240 - 7928 NORD CENTRE HIGHWAY
SURREY, B.C.
V3W 5A2

To whom it may concern:

À qui de droit:

The records of Citizenship Registration have been searched and with the information provided, no record can be located of

À partir des renseignements que vous avez fournis, les recherches faites dans les dossiers de l'enregistrement de la citoyenneté n'ont rien révélé qui indique que

Family name-Nom de famille	Given names-Prénoms
ISHERWOOD	THOMAS

Date of birth-Date de naissance			Country of birth-Pays de naissance
Y-A	M	D-J	
1938	12	23	BIRMINGHAM ENGLAND

having a pending application for or having been granted or issued a certificate of naturalization or Canadian citizenship.

aurait une demande en suspens ou qu'un certificat de naturalisation ou de citoyenneté lui aurait été attribué ou délivré.

for L. Carl
Registrar of Canadian Citizenship-Greffier de la citoyenneté canadienne

Canadä

MCC 3-29 (91-01)

FAIRBRIDGE FARM SCHOOLS
(INCORPORATED)

SAVOY HOUSE, 115 STRAND, LONDON, W.C.2

PRESIDENT: H.R.H. The Duke of Gloucester, K.G., K.T.   CHEQUES & ORDERS Payable Fairbridge Farm
CHAIRMAN : Sir Charles Hambro, K.B.E., M.C.   Schools, Inc., crossed "Westminster Bank Ltd."
GENERAL SECRETARY: Gordon Green   TELEPHONE: Temple Bar 6708

R.Plemderleith Esq.
Middlemore.

6th May
1947

Dear Mr.Plemderleith,

Thomas Isherwood.

We confirm that arrangements will be
made to include Tom in the party of boys due to leave
for the Prince of Wales Fairbridge Farm School,
Vancouver Island, by the "Aquitania", on May 19.

Yours sincerely,

General Secretary

COMMUNICATIONS should be addressed to the General Secretary at the Society's Headquarters

Middlemore
EMIGRATION HOMES

CROWLEY HOUSE · WEOLEY PARK ROAD · SELLY OAK · BIRMINGHAM · 29

TELEPHONES:
SECRETARY—SELLY OAK 0021
MATRON—SELLY OAK 1244

19 APR 1950

18th April, 1950.

W.R.Vaughan Esq.,
The Fairbridge Society,
London. W.14.

Dear Mr. Vaughan,

I am specially interested
just now on the report on Tommy Isherwood
which Mr. Plows has sent through. There
is no doubt the boy is in a first class home
with Mr. and Mrs. Lovick.

Yours sincerely,

Secretary & Superintendent.

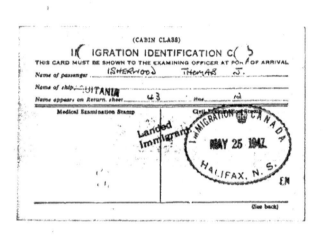

In 1992, I learned I was not a Canadian Citizen, and again in 1997 the records were not corrected. I had to gain proof that I was shipped to Canada at the age of 8. There was no record. I had to dig deeper and luckily learned of Middlemore Emigration Homes in England, who I wrote and after some time received the documents proving that I had indeed received landed immigration at the age of 8, May 25th, 1947. A copy of those confirmation documents were forwarded to Canadian Immigration. In 1998, I again enquired to Immigration Canada, and I appeared in the immigration records as landed in Halifax in 1947. I still had to complete the application to become a Canadian Citizen.

Further to our conversation of September 16, 1997, I would like to take this opportunity to once more address the issue of Mr. Tom Isherwood's citizenship. Although both the Citizenship and Immigration Acts contain provisions which must legally be met before citizenship may be granted, we try to deal with unusual cases, within those constraints, as sympathetically as possible.

In order to obtain Canadian citizenship, Mr. Isherwood will have to complete and submit an application for citizenship under Section 5(1) of the *Citizenship Act*, which governs who may apply for citizenship. Mr. Isherwood's application for citizenship will then be processed at our National Headquarters in Ottawa in order to ensure an expeditious review.

As this individual has been living in Canada for many years time but no record that Mr. Isherwood was landed when he arrived in 1947 exists, we will invoke Section 2(2)(b) of the Citizenship Act and deem him to have been landed. Mr. Isherwood will therefore not have to pay the cost-recovery fees associated with the immigration process.

I would also like to mention that, if Mr. Isherwood is 60 years of age or older at the time that a Citizenship judge evaluates his application, the *Citizenship Regulations* allow us to waive the language and knowledge requirements which are usually associated with the application. Thus, he would not have to write the citizenship test.

I have included an application for citizenship with this letter. Please ask Mr. Isherwood to complete this application and send it to the following address with the required fee, photographs and documentation:

    Citizenship and Immigration Canada
    Citizenship Case Review
    Attn: Rosemarie Redden
    Ottawa, Ontario
    K1A 1L1

../2

The Best I Remember – A Cruel British Tragedy

Citizenship and Immigration Canada   Citoyenneté et Immigration Canada

Our File
Notre référence

Re: **Objet:**

In reply to your inquiry of
this is to advise that the following particulars of entry
appear in the Immigration Records:

En réponse à votre demande de renseignements en date du   voici les indications qui figurent dans les dossiers de l'immigration relativement à l'admission de la personne susnommée

Name   ISHERWOOD, THOMAS J.   *Nom*

Name of Vessel   S.S. AQUITANIA   *Nom du navire*

Port of Arrival HALIFAX, N.S.   Date 25/05/1947   *Port d'arrivée*   *Date*

Date of Birth or Age   8   YEARS OLD   *Date de naissance ou âge*

Status   LANDED IMMIGRANT   *Statut*

Accompanied by   *Accompagné(e) de*

Remarks   *Observations*
SAILING FROM: SOUTHAMPTON MAY 20, 1947.
BORN: BIRMINGHAM, ENG. DEST. TO: W.J.
GARNETT, ESQ., PRINCIPAL, PRINCE OF WALES
FAIRBRIDGE FARM SCHOOL, COWICHAN STATION,
VANC. ISLAND, B.C. NEAREST RELATIVE OUTSIDE
CANADA: FAIRBRIDGE FARM SCHOOLS(INC.) SAVOY
HOUSE, 115 STRAND, LONDON, ENGLAND.

Head, Query Response Centre (Immigration Officer)
Le chef, Centre des demandes de renseignements (agent d'immigration)

June 4, 1998
Date

Canada

19th December 1945.

Miss E. Brideoake,
Jervoise Road Infants School,
Wooley Castle.

Dear Miss Brideoake,

The correct dates of birth of
the two Isherwood children are -

Jean Isherwood   25.9.37
Thomas Isherwood 25.12.38

Best wishes for Christmas and

the New Year.

Yours sincerely,

Secretary &
Superintendent.

Letter from Margaret, my sister:

….. *What I remember about Dad. He was a very quiet man, very smart. Could talk about anything and was very musical. He could play a lot of musical instruments. It must have been in 1942 when you and Joe were taken away. Beryl was already in hospital and I was due to go into hospital. You and Joe were there when I went to bed, but both of you were gone when I woke up next morning. Dad asked Mum where you were. And I remember they had a big argument. But he never found out where you had gone. I cannot remember Jane being home at the time. When I went into hospital Dad came to see me but not Mum. No one knew where you and Joe went. The first place was not to Middlemore. Lots of kids were taken as evacuees where most went to homes in the country, fostered out to institutions. I know both Mum and Dad tried to find you after the war. But were never told where you were.*

We now know you were sent to Middlemore and then to Canada. Joe of course ended up in Australia but was supposed to go with you to Canada. Dad died December 1947. Mum and he had already split. She was with Baker as his housekeeper from 1944 on. She found out in 48 or 49 that you had gone to Canada and had been adopted to a Dr. and Mrs. Childs. But they should have got her signature before they could adopt. She was also told that Joe was in Australia and that he had TB which of course he didn't. Well Tom see if you can gather any info from what I have written. It's pretty hard because everything is a jumble in my mind. If you need any more I will try to work my brain harder. Did you know our Granddad was younger than our Dad? So Dad lied about his age when he married Mum. Check his marriage certificate against his death certificate and work it out. If he was 43 in 1932, How could he have been 74 in 1947. See what I mean. Love Margaret xxxx

PRINCE OF WALES FAIRBRIDGE FARM SCHOOL
COWICHAN STATION
near Duncan
BRITISH COLUMBIA

1st December 1947.

G. C. Warnock, Esq.,
Assistant Secretary,
Fairbridge Farm Schools Inc.,
Savoy House, 115 Strand,
London, W.C.2, England.

Dear George Warnock,

<u>Thomas Isherwood.</u>

Further to our correspondence regarding the Isherwood family, may we know the family circumstances surrounding the placement of the children at Middlemore Homes in the first place? Does the mother or the father keep in touch with any of the children? Would Tommy's letter to his mother reach her c/o Middlemore? How old a girl would Beryl Hazel be?

Tommy is a fine little chap and it would be a help in working with him to know something of the family circumstances and his relationship with his family.

Yours sincerely,

Principal.

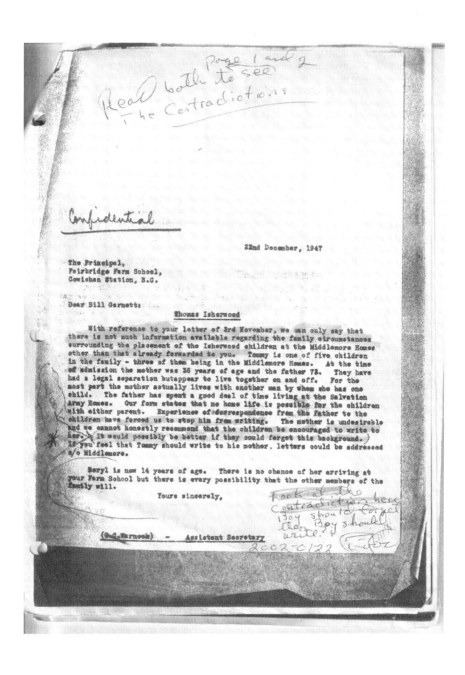

THE FAIRBRIDGE SOCIETY

(INCORPORATED)

CREAGH HOUSE, 38 HOLLAND VILLAS ROAD, LONDON, W.14

The following .... Report, dated .... April, 1955

has been received from ...... PRINCE OF WALES FAIRBRIDGE FARM SCHOOL, B.C.

Name ...... TOMMY ISHERWOOD .... Date of Birth 23.12.38 Sailing Date 20.5.47

Extract from Report on Fairbridgians interviewed
by Mr. Larnder during April, 1955.

Last year Tommy spent his holidays working on a small farm
in Pitt Meadows, owned by Mrs. M. Skelton. He enjoyed farm work
and liked the district, and at the end of the summer expressed
a wish to stay there. Unfortunately, towards the end of the year,
Mrs. Skelton's health failed, and it became necessary for Tommy to
be moved to the house of Mr. Gray, a neighbouring farmer. I
called at his home and Mrs. Gray told me that he was helping Mr.
Skelton during the Easter holidays. It was at this home that
I found him. Both Mrs. Gray and Mrs. Skelton spoke well of
Tommy, I had a long talk with the latter while waiting for the
lad to come in from the farm. Tommy is in Grade 10 at the local
High School. He is a bright boy and, according to reports, doing
well at school. He is not tall but carries himself well; he is
a very nice boy to meet, has a pleasant manner and way of speaking.
He is very like his Fairbridge chum, Barry Sutton, with whom he
was anxious to re-establish contact. His address is:-

                    c/o Mrs. Gray,
                        Pitt Meadows, B.C.

C C
 O O
 P P
 Y

Social Welfare Branch,
 Field Service,
Municipal Hall, Box 190.
Haney, B. C.
 August 12th, 55.

Child Welfare Division,

Parliament Buildings,

Victoria, B. C.

Re: ISHERWOOD, Elsie & William,
 Ch: Thomas Isherwood,
 b. 23.12.38
 c/o Mr. & Mrs. Guy Marshall,
 2nd Ave., Hammond, B. C.

This is further to our memo dated July 7th on the above boy, Tommy has continued his job on the C.P.R. and his monthly earnings are approximately $265.00. The company has held back two weeks pay but the boy was able to pay $30.00 at the end of July to Mrs. Marshall so we are recommending that $30.00 be paid to Mrs. Marshall by our department bringing the total for July to $60.00. This being the amount agreed upon when the placement was made.

Working has been a good experience for Tommy. He certainly looks healthy, is well tanned and seems to get along well with his employers. At every opportunity we encourage the boy to return to school this Fall and we believe that Tommy will, although right now he has stated that he is undecided. His main goal at the present time is to buy an old model car as this will supply him with transportation to and from his job and give him an opportunity to try out his mechanical ability by tinkering with his care in the evenings. With this in mind Tommy has saved every penny that he can get his hands on. He refuses to pay bus fare to and from work as he would rather hitch hike because it saves a few cents. He has stopped going to picture shows altogether because they cost too much and he has sold his bicycle to another one of our wards for $34.00 and will bank this money as soon as the money is received.

We have discussed carefully with Tommy the responsibilities of owning and driving a car and have cautioned him that he must not drive without a license. We particularly wanted to know how he was going to manage to operate a car if he went back to school this Fall and Tommy replied to this by saying that he wanted a car so badly he could find ways and means of operating it. He would get a part time job or at least a job on the weekends and he promised to pay what he could towards his board.

We have hesitated to pursue Tommy's request for a driver's license for several months because we did not feel we knew him well enough to make a recommendation. We feel now that the boy has such a strong desire to drive that he may drive whether he has a license or not and because he will soon be seventeen and is moving towards independence we are recommending that an application for a minor's driver's license be granted. The partially completed application form is enclosed and if you approve would you please return the completed form to us as soon as possible.

.................2

c.c. Fairbridge Farm School
 Cowichan Station, B. C.   26.8.55.

The Best I Remember – A Cruel British Tragedy

– 2 –

We realize there may be an emotional basis for Tommy's strong desire
to own and operate his own car but we feel that we should try to meet this
need and yet give the lad as much protection as we can (driver's license, and
maximum insurance coverage) and perhaps when Tommy discovers that the costs of
operating a car are pretty high, he may be able to relinquish the idea for the
time being. On the other hand the boy does have some mechanical ability and we
would like to see this developed. We had in mind an apprenticeship this
Fall at Mussallem's Garage if we can not keep Tommy at school.

Thank you for your consideration in this case.

Bruce E. McLean,
Social Worker.

BEM:ls

Encls.
"A.O. Morrison for"
(Mrs.) B. Leydier,
District Supervisor.

Social Welfare Branch,
HANEY, B. C.

Child Welfare Division,
Victoria, B. C. August 26, 55.

AUG 29 1955

Re: ISHERWOOD, Elsie and William
Ch: Thomas John ISHERWOOD
b. 23.12.38

Thank you for your report on Tommy. You have had quite a hand full of difficult teen-age problems in your area recently - and we are sure it is gratifying to you to see a lad like Tom do well in a $265 a month job. We were quite amused by his great interest in saving his money. Hope he keeps up the good work.

We note you asked us on June 3rd to explore with Children's Aid Society the possibility of Tom returning to the home of Mrs. Mona Childs of Surrey. We wrote to them on June 16th but have heard nothing since. We wonder if you have heard direct from that Agency. From your memorandum of August 12th, we imply that you intend to keep Tom in his present boarding home with Mrs. Marshall. Would you advise us please if you wish us to follow up on our memorandum to Children's Aid Society of June 16th regarding placing Tom with Mrs. Childs, or not.

As per your recommendation we are forwarding a cheque to Mrs. Marshall for $30, for maintenance for the month of July, and understand that Tom has paid her the balance of $30 for the same month. May we be advised please as to what arrangement is to be made for the month of August? First, if Tom continues on in his present employment, we assume he can undertake full responsibility for board and room as of the first of August. If he returns to school, we expect you will be recommending we assume full responsibility as of the first of September and share it for August. If he takes an apprenticeship we would like to know what he will earn (we believe it amounts to about $70 per month for the first six months) and what he can contribute toward his board and room out of that.

We have given consideration to Tom's request for permission to obtain a driver's licence, and hesitate to give it at this time, because of his extreme youth. Also, there is no need for Tom to have a licence at this point to maintain employment, and, as you have already pointed out to him, there is the question of up-keep particularly if he returns to school. We whole heartedly approve of Tom investing some of his savings in an old car, if he wishes, to have in the backyard an tinker around with, but we wonder if you could persuade him to forego driving for a few more months. Say we make the granting of permission to obtain a licence as a sort of seventeenth birthday gift? At this point, we do not know whether Tom can already drive a car, or if he has some reliable male we can count

- 2 -

on to teach him and help him make his first ventures out with
it. If he were in a regular foster home with an interested
father, we would feel a bit different about granting him this
privilege, but being quite on his own at sixteen and one half
places an awful lot of responsibility on a boy.

Please discuss this again with Tom. Assure him we would be quite
pleased to see him go ahead and get himself an old car to work
on, and if he could refrain from driving until he is a bit older
we would agree to his getting a licence when he is seventeen.

Ruby McKay,
Superintendent of
Child Welfare.

P.Harrison:iv

Encl.

c.c. Fairbridge Farm School
Cowichan Station, B. C.   26.8.55.

Fairbridge Farm School Photo
Tom Isherwood first row, second in from the left. The shortest fellow.

Barry Hagen (standing) and Tom Isherwood (sitting) playing on Tom's $3.00 sleigh — a present from his Godfather

I wished I had connected again with Barry. I remember asking about him, but never connected again. At Fairbridge Farm Schools when we woke in the morning some of our friends would be gone and not heard from again.

Fairbridge Farm School, Duncan BC

Fairbridge Church

Taken at Fairbridge Farm School. Don't let our Sunday clothes fool you, it was most likely a 'dress rehearsal' for the public to see.

Pat Lovick (my sister for a short time) and Tom

The Best I Remember – A Cruel British Tragedy

Tom, age 16, Pitt Meadows B.C

Tom – Air Force

Tom and wife Sheryl, with their family

The Best I Remember – A Cruel British Tragedy

Kyra, eldest great-grandchild's graduation – family photo
Vicki is Tom and Sheryl's daughter

POETRY

I was born on December 23 or 25, 1938 in Birmingham England. I survived and grew my first years as a child as the Second World War raged on. I was placed in the loveless emigration poor homes in 1944 and cannot remember any family life.

I was sent to Canada in 1947 and placed in another home for the underprivileged. This home was situated on 1000 acres of land where no matter how big or small, old or young, you learned to work. You accepted the hard loveless discipline as you knew no other way. Leaving my tin dishes behind I left the Farm to be devoured in a stream of foster homes.

I grew up quickly as a survivor, cold for the lack of affection, and at 15 was on my own. At 23 I married my wife Sheryl, and we will celebrate fifty-nine years of marriage December 14. We have beautiful children and now grand-children and great-grandchildren.

In my sixties I learned of and found my siblings who were sent to Australia. Siblings I forgot I even had. I suffered a complete loss of childhood thanks to the English and Canadian Governments.

Some of my poems reflect the sadness of my past and express the foolishness of war and the heartache that follows. All of them tell a story from my heart, and I will carry on with my newfound love.

The Smoky Dusty Dawn

Through dense smoke and fires of a worn torn dawn
I hear a faint baby cry that sounds forlorn.
Sadness and tears filled my eyes and I pray to God to clear the skies.
Why is man allowed to trash, such little ones, dare I ask.
On hands and knees I felt my way, not knowing about landmines
Or where they lay.
Through the rubble and craters left by bombs
A lone bird was singing, a very sad song.
Perspiration and fear on my face, did not deter me in my haste.
I found the baby that had cried, in a bombed out orphanage
Where the rest have died.
If God has a Kingdom, as some say maybe
Then dear Lord help me save this baby.

Along Time Ago – In the British Isles

Along time ago in the British Isles war reached on over thousands of miles
Hundreds of children were displaced, separated forever in total disgrace
Their dates of birth and names were changed
Put in homes to be re arranged.
Little did we know what horror waited
Your turn would come and you were gated
Brothers or sisters how would I know
Could be in the bomb shelter with me below.
Tin dishes and rations on a plate could not match the sadness or their fate.
Little faces cold as stone, never knew we would not go home.
Discipline was cruel and so unjust
Some kids would cry till their heart would bust
A few of us survived this cruel ordeal, there was no love and none to steal.
On a great troop ship I sailed the north Atlantic
It was rough and some more were frantic.
It did not bother my young soul; my tiny heart was full of holes.
Being shipped alone to a foreign land, I learned survival and took a stand.
I did not know the feel or meaning of love
So I put my faith in the man above.
By the age of ten I became a man, hard outside but soft as a lamb.
I still have trouble with the word called love
The man never replied from high above.
Over sixty-years have now gone by, a lonesome tear still clouds my eyes.
I am not as lonely as I was; I don't look for my mummy in the stars.
The answer missing in my life, is how your own kind created such strife.
One day I may know, and one day you people will be judged as well.

War Now Behind Him

A War now behind him, and life in disarray
The boy is tiny and out muscled today.
The little boy is not mature enough to know that the future
Is going to be tough.
He sailed across the sea to a distant land
On a rusty ship under strict command.
Boy ate from tin dishes and rang a train bell
I'm either Oliver Twist or I am living in hell.
No mummy or daddy he had been told far away
No brothers or sisters to play in the day.
Time passed by, for the little Lad, emotional stability was not to be had.
At times he had many tears and he cried
Why am I not the apple in somebody's eye?
He was never one to be suicidal but he wonders about parents
Who were never his idol.
To the people that were mean, some looked after this tot
I hope you are in hell where surely you will rot.
Boy latched onto many friends, but many times his memory would bend.
God spoke to me many years from aloft
I have always known he loves me a lot.
When I get to heaven he guarantees me a spot.
No more sadness, no more fear, finally I can shed more tears.

Journey of Life for a Child Migrant

The starting line was on a British shore
Where this young boy witnessed every day of war.
After the war he was put on a boat, so rat infested, would it float?
Aquitania was her name, third largest troop ship on the mane.
Across the rough and stormy sea, the North Atlantic is all he could see.
There was no fear in the boy's blue eyes
As he ran the decks to much surprise.
He was a happy little boy from all reports
And for his size was good at sports.
Little did he know like a log that is hollow
His child's mind would learn of sorrow.
Like a pilgrim sailing to a foreign land, no love or guidance even from God
What an awful childhood the boy trod.
On the move from home to home like a Nomad he would roam.
Many obstacles in the way, he would run the gauntlet many a day.
As boy matured and grew, he heard about things he never knew.
Things that were cruel and out of place
He was disgusted and hurt by this disgrace.
Shipped from loved ones who don't understand to a foreign country
A distant land.
Through fun and laughter, hardship and terror
The boy would survive the northern weather.
For all those creeps who cannot make it right, you will answer to God
Who will decide your plight.

Curtains of Heaven

The curtains of Heaven were opened today
God look down from his window above
At all his creatures created with love.
Three Angels pass by, one playing the harp
They were playing tag in God's beautiful park
The gates stood solid on the righteous path
And were only open to let people pass
On the inside it has been said, people awoke from a deep sleep in their bed.
God realized he had made mistakes
Some of the desert could have been lakes.
People had been made from different moulds
With different colors and different clothes.
People were not put on earth to fight and God wished they would not
With all his might.
On the path of love and life, sometimes things got over bearing,
But it was not God that was not caring.
God had done all he can, but sometimes worried about creating man.
Without pomp and a lot of glory, people come here to tell their story.
Twelve white doves went flying by and God closed the window in the sky.
Another day had come to pass, he welcomed more children home at last.

Atlantic Ocean – Dreams and Shattered Emotions

This is my story of the Atlantic Ocean, which carried dreams
And shattered emotions.
If only all her stories could be told, of adventure and conquests of war
As mighty ships sailed from shore to shore.
Long after the big war was over my turn came
To board the Aquitania, third largest troop ship on the Maine.
The tremendous size of this tired lady had my mind aghast
As little boats pushed and pointed her from the harbor at last.
Still colored in gray to match the sea and fog
Her four funnels pointing skyward giving thanks to God
Aquitania made her way to sea under a skillful captain I would never see.
I listened to creaks and unfamiliar sounds as the funnels belched black
There was no turning back.
The ship that had loomed large in the eyes of this boy
Now bobbed in the ocean like a little toy.
A vicious wind came up and the sea looked angry
The waves thrashed the ship on its watery trail, and made this boy
Scared, sick, and pale.
I had never witnessed such natural power
Where even the bravest men would cower.
Below deck reserved for orphans and water rats in our cramped space
I suppose we did not belong to the human race.
The voyage seemed endless to this little boy in his home on the ocean
Not a tear did he shed or show any emotion.
I just can't remember much of the crossing, but the name Aquitania
I do think of often.
My country of birth got rid of us tainted tissue
But now being older I seek the truth.
Much later in life as the story unfolded.
I was not the orphan and my heart exploded.
I was exiled from England across this ocean
To a foreign port in Nova Scotia.
I had no family to tell me stories or share their love
A government cover-up is still ongoing
To hide the horror of the story above.

First Christmas in Canada 1947

I was six years old when I tried to sleep
The room was dark, and there wasn't a peep.
Christmas Eve was here at last, in my new country that is so vast.
I hung a darned woolen sock at the foot of my old iron bed
One blanket, and no pillow for my tiny head.
Pictures of war played in my mind.
A gruesome reminder that I could have died.
My first Christmas in Canada in nineteen forty-seven
The dormitory is quiet like it must be in heaven.
Rhythmic soft breathing of other little boys, some dreams of magical toys.
As morning came with broken sleep, I had not counted many sheep.
I fumbled quietly in the dark, a strange feeling in my heart.
My sock had gone from the end of the bed, and fear set in
That Santa is dead.
Silently I lay in bed, tears of sadness I did shed.
Outside I went and scanned the skies
And I prayed that Santa had not crashed and died.
To my family that abandoned me, you broke my heart till eternity.
Elders tried to make me understand
Santa hadn't changed my address in this great land.
Man is born equal, so it's said
Tell that to the orphan in the iron bed.

In a Far off Land

In a far-off land across the sea, a baby boy was born
With no chance you see.
Rivers were raging and flowing in blood
Bombs poured down from the skies above.
The lad was a veteran at three years old
Living in bomb shelters trying to be bold.
There was no time during battle to scold
As one did not know when our home would explode.
The sounds of war were stamped in his brain
Would he live to see the sun again
The boy was taught to believe in God, holding the good book
He started to nod. Then one day there were no more sirens, fires or noise,
Children were searching for burnt out toys.
Boy ended up on a big ship one day
In the middle of the ocean he could play.
The Aquitania was the name of the ship, a battle-scarred lady
Kept me safe on this trip.
Happy at the time but how could I know
The cruelty I would suffer from adults below.
Years have gone by and I do reflect, nobody wanted me, I thought by heck.
This is not entirely true - my wife of forty years might argue with you.

Winds of War

Another year has slipped by and Remembrance Day is here at last.
The winds of war that were blowing softly
Have now erupted and could be costly.
Peoples fear soon turn to a tear as the drums of war get nearer and near.
Love ones leave against all their might, to fight a war that is out of sight.
Weapons of destruction that were sitting idle
Put fear in people that are now our rival.
No matter where the conflict lay, men should think for another day.
Whoever thinks they are supreme commander
Should listen to the world and stop the anger.
Save the children it has been said, but they only grow up to fight instead.
If the truth be known about this earth, man does not own
The thing called dirt.
If man keeps going on this course of action
This tiny planet will have a huge reaction.
Color won't matter, neither will money.
Religion will be gone and there will be lust
God help us now as there will be no trust.
Machines of war will rust and all God's people returned to dust.

One Day When I Was Feeling Low

One day when I was feeling low
I thought of Flanders Field where poppies grow.
As my mind reflected on the past, an invisible cloud appeared
And held me fast.
Flames seared my heart and burnt my soul; I shook like jelly in a bowl.
With shaky knees I asked God to set me free
I heard no answer just the whimper of me.
Along time ago the adult war ended
But many children were left unattended.
Family failed to return from war, no home coming through my door.
The message said that Dad was dead, I sobbed and cried in my iron bed.
It was easier to face life as I got older, the truth was hidden
And I became bolder.
I asked for naught and was cut no slack
I was exiled from my homeland and never looked back.
Now I am older and have made late family ties
I have no thanks for the country that lied.
My brother and sisters were sent far away by sea
Without the chance to know their brother me.
Yes an adult war had nearly done us in, but hard to break the bond of kin.
No words of kindness will cross my lips
For those shameful few who should have served the Hood, a battleship.
My tears won't come as they grow old, but God will help one day I'm told.

War is Hell! Next Door to Hell

Little children have no choice, they cannot speak they have no voice.
Save the children is heard around the world, the end result is so absurd.
From day one a child of war, is asking God to close the door
To shut out the ugly sounds of war.
For in God's kingdom I felt safe, with mankind I had no faith.
The noise of guns that shook a nation, countries torn in devastation.
Down the path of life this child grows, which branches off in many rows.
War is futile in the end: the only losers are loved ones and friends.
The world was started not by man, who has started wars since time began.
Violent claps of deadly thunder, have mankind finally put us under?
The end result will tell the story, as nature strips man of his former glory.

I Will Never Forget, They Won't Let Me

Remembrance Day has gone by again
A day to remember from way back then.
Is one day enough to remember when
Before your time we lost gallant men.
I remember nineteen-forty-five
The atomic bomb took many lives.
Men and women scattered over land and sea would not come back
To children like me.
I have many thoughts this special day and tend to think in a different way.
For those of you who feel no sorrow and don't understand
Pray to God for your freedom and land.
As a child I witnessed the horror of war, and every day I look
Through the freedom door.
Children took a severe licking, but some of us just keep on ticking.
It was not me to reason why, my family was sent beyond the sky.
I am a forgotten child veteran of war
But stayed in my homeland to tend the store.
The noise of war with different sounds
Gave direction to go underground.
Governments this very day, hope I die and go away.

Remembrance Day

Remembrance Day has just gone by, tears still damp in many an eye.
The shocking thing about this special day
More Veterans have left to fade away.
My memory of war is clouded some
But I remember soldiers and their guns.
One thing that bothers me the most, no mention of children
As if they were ghosts.
Thousands of children would never play as men of war took that away.
Children had no say in all great wars
Machines of war blew down their doors.
Families broken ceased to exist, children grew up with no hugs or a kiss.
Another tragedy this eleventh day, more talk of war that's on the way.
To the younger people I will say,
Teach your children about Remembrance Day.
War is hell, believe me it is so, I am living proof of what war has done.

Never Forget the Forgotten Children of War

A two minute silence would be observed around the world
At the 11th hour on this 11th day the 11th month of every year.
The mist rose slowly in the early dawn
Leaving dew drops glistening on manicured lawns.
White crosses and poppies come to mind
Mixed with sadness in a child's mind
A special day this would be, to thank the veterans that kept us free.
The only sounds are heart beats in the chest
As comrades remember who gave their best.
Standing quietly feeling sad and alone
Minds flood with memories of those who never came home.
As the Bugle sounds one more time
Remember those who gave or put life on the line.
One historical battle sadly forgotten on Remembrance Day
Are the unmentioned veteran children, exiled from family far away.
I am one child of war that lost it all, why do children take a lifetime fall?
Adults failed to keep me safe after wars end
This orphans war will never end.

Raindrops

Where do raindrops come from, I think I know.
They are from a higher power, I think it's so.
Along time ago when the earth was being made
The Creator took rest in heavenly shade.
Under the young Oak Tree, God found some comfort
But the earth was brown, even when the sun went down.
God put his mind under urgent strain and just in time he came up with rain.
The sun was hot and near boiling
The rain saved his artwork which was spoiling.
He made the sea and oceans blue, green grass appeared for me and you.
Now that God felt much better he remodeled man to share his plan.
He created tears for all mankind
To help ward off sadness on the life-line climb.
Tears are the image of raindrops it's been said
To ease one's mind on sad events.
So when the rain falls, followed by thunder, there is a greater power.

Christmas Comes in its Final Approach

As Santa looks up into the wintry night.
He worries about children mixed up in man's latest fight.
The sound of distant drums around the land
Make it impossible to take a stand.
Santa looked in the mirror in total dismay
Rudolph with his nose so bright, will not guide my sleigh that night.
Man has really no-one to thank,
I will deliver the children's toys in my army tank.
Wars are slow and food banks low, employment insurance is no way to go.
People are taxed and plenty are axed
And no way on earth they can say Ho, Ho.
Politicians sing carols as they stand at the trough
While poor homeless people get their first winter cough.
Open up your pockets and give back that raise
This may frighten people who would be amazed.
Santa will try his best without his sled
And God will be co-pilot in the tank instead.
Even Santa's wonderful tradition, with mankind's help
Could be the final edition.

My Own Soldier Poem

A fine young soldier lay bleeding in a cave
Without help soon he would join the brave
Who had taken their last breath in this clammy cave.
To stave off fear and all the rodents, he turned to God in a tender moment.
He thought of Mum and Dad miles away at home
Who would have taken his place if they had known.
His little sister she was keen and he drifted off into a pleasant dream.
He woke up suddenly and looked outside
Many strangers were after his hide.
All of a sudden, out of the blue, aircraft appeared, and they were fitting too.
It seemed like eternity but that's not so
Enemy tanks and men were on the go.
Medics appeared and one said son
Hang in there we will get you home to your mum.
You were talking in a delirious state, we know all about your sister Kate.
The war is over for you my son.
You will never have to hear the sound of another gun.

No Choice for Children

Mummy, what is war, the little girl said
As the blood seeped through her bandaged head.
Her Mummy replied, now hush now child
It is war when man goes wild.
What does that mean the child said
As she kneeled at the remains of her iron bed.
Well men have come from a far-off land
To take our oil below the sand.
Dust sifted down from the bombed-out shack
That was their home till the thunderous attack.
Remained but toppled clay bricks
It resembled the game of pick-up sticks.
Daddy's gone, but where's my brother the little girl asked
Her mummy wept at this awful task.
God took him away her mummy replied
He lives in God's house beyond the sky.
Finally her tiny head did nod as she said her prayers in front of God.
Little did their innocence know
They would join the brother in God's front row.

Horror of Unforgiving Slaughter

Invader tanks clattered through the desert sand
Churning up this barren land.
Invader aircraft controlled the skies, but to the world was no surprise.
Missiles came from out of site, through the darkness of the night.
Explosions rocked and lit the sky; many people would surely die.
Innocent children do not deserve this cruel attack.
To liberate not obliterate was the invaders aim
Should bow their heads in mortal shame.
All the pomp and all the glory, to beat a flea is another story.
Even slaughter is measured in dollars
Like vicious Pit Bulls, some men need collars.
As I write my humble entry, I think of my war in another century.
When the dust settles, and the smoke is gone
Man will be planning for another one.

Children Running Scared

Children running scared, with bombs of death falling out of the air.
They are too young to understand the foreign invaders in their land.
Little ones can't ask parents what's going on
They were killed with the blast from bombs.
All alone in the place called home
Now a bombed out shelter they would have to roam.
No water to drink or food to eat, two tiny children forced out on the street.
Liberation they had no idea, with Army troops they would live in fear.
The little boy's arm was sore limp, he wanted Mummy
And something to drink.
His younger sister made their way through rubble
If she didn't find help they were deep in trouble.
A big machine appeared in sight
And they could not hide in this bright light.
The giant machine came to a screeching halt
A soldier jumped out and said c'mon.
They hugged each other and cried out loud
As they were given food and water, with the rest of the crowd.
The giant machine went on its way
And the children were left alone for another day.
All in all, it is not well, their tiny young lives have a taste of hell.

Higher Than the Mountains

Higher than the mountain, far above the trees
On the way to heaven with a soft gentle breeze.
As I look down from my magical flight
I wonder if mankind will ever get it right.
The world below is a mess, as God will confess
Mankind has failed a simple test.
The sea below have no fish, birds are gone, their song is lost
What have we done and at what cost.
As I ponder the time gone by, is it for me to reason why?
All God's creatures big and small had no chance of standing tall.
In the recipe that created earthly man, one thing was missing or overlooked,
Man was not born equal as written in the book.
A last look down from heaven above at a world now gone
That man should have loved.
It is too late now, no turning back, no more countries to attack
No more next time or another chance, no more people will sing or dance.
To the nation that wanted it all, your punishment will be greater than all.

Path of Life

The path of life can be hard to trudge, with heart and mind
So full of sludge.
There is no garage for minor repair
And some live their lives in great despair.
Some people are born to be destitute, their journey through life is absolute.
Man is born equal is just a myth, look around and take a whiff.
Some are born with a golden spoon
While others are born in doom and gloom.
Live your life the best you can, you are just as good as fellow man.
At the end it may sound crude, but you take your path completely nude.
There you stand equal at last, much different now than in the past.
There is no-one that hears the sound of the bell
As the ringing in your head sends you straight to hell.

Mother Nature is Supreme Commander

Mother Nature took inventory this New Years Day
And looked over her garden in total dismay.
Enough is enough she cried out loud
Thunder could be heard behind the clouds.
Those ignorant beings that God calls man
Keep ruining my garden as fast as they can.
From the trees in the forest and fish in the seas
There is not much left on my stock list you see.
Decision time is here, I have to act fast
With a pending war which could be the last.
I believed in God when and I took this job
But the years went by and we started to sob.
At high council in the sky, it was decided to let man die.
Man was given more chances than a cat, his last swing will come at bat.
Man mixed the recipe for his own demise
He is not greater than the Maker's tears.

Silent Running

As I came out of a silent sleep, like a submarine my thoughts ran deep.
My dream had come to a pleasant end
As the picture ended of God my friend.
With all his love and super powers
He ringed my heart with petals of many flowers.
God gave us sunshine and the rain
And a lifetime pass of riding on his holy train.
As man rode through God's garden, destroying all in his path
There would be for certain an aftermath.
As God looked from his window above, is this the man I created with love?
The Creator looked on in total shock
Should he stop this man's biological clock.
When this happens there will be no light, man will perish in lonely fright.
With really no one else to blame, man will be banished in immortal shame.
Nothing to gain in man's domain of going to war.
God took it back and closed his door.
This story goes that light years ahead with sorrow behind
God has made a new model of man that is gentle and kind.

War Mongers

A far-off land is again under a one sided vicious attack.
A dictator madman runs the show it is said
Where innocent people can lose their head.
The almighty architect who created this land
Gave extra helpings of heat and sand.
Feeling bad with this barren plan
He would make it up to this Nomadic man.
He made them camels who needed little water and set the pace
To find an oasis in this desert waste.
For good measure under the sand, God hid riches of future spoil.
Man found God's prize buried below the sand, and deep in the soil.
It was black and crude and man named it oil.
Miles away man feared a shortage of fuel
They started a war that is vicious and cruel.
The little country did not have a chance
The dictator could have been removed well in advance.
The greatest mistake the invader did not plan for
Your answer to God when you arrive at his door.
It was he that made you a super power
But when judged by him it is you who will cower.
Millions have no say in right or wrong, only sad words to put in a song.
Little children should have no strife, just like God gave them life.

A Door Marked Dreams

As I nodded off in my bed, the stress of life was leaving my head.
A door marked dreams was open a crack
Showing a ray of light mixed in with black.
A voice I recognized from the past
Was here from God's kingdom, he said was vast.
My name was called to enter the door
I was fitted with angel wings and able to soar.
No other human had made this trip and returned
But it was God's wish to share what I learned.
The peace and tranquility put my mind at ease
As we flew over places of color that were there to please.
Like autumn leaves on earthly trees, a softness rocked me in a gentle breeze.
I was told of the tunnel and the bright light
The journey I took was not one of fright.
As I looked from above at this Garden of Eden
People were happy no one was thieving.
Daylight on earth was coming we were advised
I left the kingdom with teary eyes.
As I awoke to meet the day, was that a dream or real I pray.
No one on earth will believe my story this I know
But in my heart, I know it is so.
When I leave this planet, I go in glory without fright
To remember my dream of this wonderful night.

Eagle

Way up high on a mountain peak, a glint of sun bounced off a golden beak.
With wings spread wide, I could have cried
At the magnificent splendor God supplied.
There was a hush and then a rush, as the eagle put herself into a dive
toward the mighty river Clyde.
The salmon she clutched was a little bit much
As her wings beat their way to the sky.
It was an honour to behold and my duty to share
This spectacle taken in the air.
As the eagle gained altitude toward her nest, only a picture could tell it best.
The razor talons that clutched the salmon
As it perched on the nest in a dangerous cavern.
The young took over and Mum moved over
And she looked at her babies with pride.
It was now feast or famine as they clawed at the salmon
For without Mummy they would die.
I was humbled to say the least, to watch Golden Eagles have such a feast.
The wind was blowing and it started snowing
Inside my heart was glowing as I could not believe this day.
A spectacular sight was shared with me
And hoped my story would go down in history.

The Babbling Brook – 2001

The water runs clear in the babbling brook
As I fish for trout with my shiny hook.
The trees bend over from the weight of the snow
And glisten their reflection on the pools below.
The mountains rise with magnificent splendor
The snowcapped peaks I shall remember.
When I think back so long ago, was there a reason I had to go.
Nowhere on earth is such a pretty place
To ask forgiveness before such grace.
The time will come and I shall return
When they scatter my ashes from the urn.
But for now I must be off, as the plane waits to take me aloft.
I got in the car and had a last look
I shall always remember the babbling brook.
Out in a field a short distance away
It looked like deer eating the farmers hay.
It was so picturesque my eyes would not leave
Like a beautiful painting in make believe.
The male deer was called a Buck and its velvety horns, had me awestruck.
A beautiful female was called a Doe
And made sounds like music from long ago.
I started the car and was soon out of sight
What a beautiful ending to a beautiful sight.
My plane left the ground as I looked out the window
And heart felt memories brought on a warm glow.
As the airplane cuts through the darkness and snow
It won't be so long before I come back you know,

Poem of Hope

I staggered along a forest trail, frail and thin, separated from all my kin.
Days and nights had now gone by when I heard a sound
From beyond the sky.
It was faint and muffled to my ears, but brought on hope and many tears.
I made my way through bush and brambles
Oblivious to cuts and scratches as I rambled.
Out of nowhere came a clearing, the silver sand was so appealing.
The sound had directed me from the trees and to the sea
A ship was coming just for me.
How and why I will never know
But my heart was on fire with eternal glow.
After time when my body got well, I had a story I would tell.
To make the world a better place, relax a little and change the pace
Hug your family every day, you never know when love will be taken away.
For neighbors and strangers too, be kind to them
And they will be kind to you.
A blink in the eye is all we are, our journey is short but appears so far.

Dog

On a dark and wintry night, with a lonely Star as my guiding light.
Such a short time ago, I had left my vehicle stuck in snow.
On each side of the forestry road, the eerie sounds
Made my heart grow cold.
I knew I could not stay with the car, but civilization was so far.
I plodded along and time went by, it was getting light and I wanted to cry.
The shrill distant bark of a dog came to my ears
And my cold hands wiped away the tears.
With urgency I forced my pace, I did not want to leave the human race.
I foraged on toward the sound where I prayed to God I would be found.
The now stopped falling and the sun was high
I saw the dog, I would not die.
With tail wagging and eyes so soft
He guided me to sleep in a warm hay loft.
Then it was off again with the dog I called Love
Sent to me by the man above.

Happy 94th Birthday – Dedicated to my First Adopted Mum

From overseas came a young English boy
Without a Mum or Dad or even a toy.
The boy had survived an endless war
And ended up on a foreign shore.
The lad lived on an island so far from home
It had one thousand acres for him to roam.
He had a Robinson Crusoe heart but did not get off
To a very good start.
Lad ate off tin dishes so it's been said
And was never canned for wetting the bed.
A young blonde lady took the boy home
Gave him a brother, a sister, and toys to play.
All seemed well in the beautiful home
But destiny was written and the boy would roam.
One-day sadness came to pass
And the boy was alone and cried aghast.
In time he got lost as in a dream
And survived to grow up strong and clean.
Strange as it seems but there was no answer
As he loved that family long ago
From many more homes he had to go.
Fifty-four years went by with no surprise
The young boy still brought a twinkle to the blonde lady's eyes.
My mum from the past is ninety-four today
Still has the energy to work and play!
I am glad she was mine for a while, so long ago
It was not my choice for me to go….

Together Again

My brother arrived in Canada, twelve thousand miles from home.
Five weeks he could visit, and surely they would roam.
Years apart had changed us, his speech was from down under
But in our hearts and actions, were not to put us under.
When we were little children, others sealed our fate.
We survived their wrath, and journey even though it's late.
His wife is a true Ozzy, and we are glad she made this trip
The years put up with my brother really makes her hip.
They left their lovely daughters and families far across the sea
But the love in our hearts will yearn for them, from here to eternity.
The days are passing quickly and the airport is not far.
When we play Slim Dusty as he strums his old guitar,
We will think of our Ozzy rellies as we gaze up at the stars

Love You

It just dawned on me about tomorrow
A day that is sweet without any sorrow.
February fourteenth I have been told, buy your honey a pot of gold.
Born some years back near the serpentine
For forty years she has been my valentine.
Makes me wonder what I would do, if I could not eat her famous stew.
All year long she cooks and cleans, patching holes in old blue jeans.
Plus the fact she works away from home
And still spends time on the telephone.
Time for grandkids, even the dog, when we were younger we liked to clog.
Sometimes the magic word is hard to say, but I will say it this special day
LLLLLLLove Y, Yooouuuu Honey

197

Manufactured by Amazon.ca
Bolton, ON